WHAT ABOUT CARRIE?

Jennifer Brown was at home, preparing to go for a swim, when she became aware of a man standing outside the front door. She could see him through the etched-glass door before she heard the doorbell ring. When she answered the door, she was confronted by a sheriff's deputy.

"Is Rita Brown here?" he asked.

"No, but I'm her daughter, Jennifer."

He told her there had been a car accident and that her sister Carrie was in it.

"Oh no, you must be mistaken," Jennifer reassured him, "Carrie's coming home on the school bus."

The deputy looked at his hand. He had used it as an emergency notepad, writing notes on it. "Do you know a Dennis Hill?"

Jennifer was beginning to experience the first signs of uneasiness. "Yes," she said.

"Mary Hill and Amy Hill?" he inquired.

Jennifer was trying hard to maintain her composure. After all, she was the big sister. Wasn't she supposed to be there for her little sister? "What about Carrie?" she asked.

"She didn't make it."

SPEED DEMON

GOLDIE GUTTENBERG

PINNACLE BOOKS
Kensington Publishing Corp.
http://www.kensingtonbooks.com

Some names have been changed to protect the privacy of individuals connected to this story.

PINNACLE BOOKS are published by

Kensington Publishing Corp.
850 Third Avenue
New York, NY 10022

All Kensington Titles, Imprints, and Distributed Lines are available at special quantity discounts for bulk purchases for sales promotions, premiums, fund-raising, and educational or institutional use. Special book excerpts or customized printings can also be created to fit specific needs. For details, write or phone the office of the Kensington special sales manager: Kensington Publishing Corp., 850 Third Avenue, New York, NY 10022, attn: Special Sales Department, Phone: 1-800-221-2647.

Pinnacle and the P logo Reg. U.S. Pat. & TM Off.

First Pinnacle Printing: October 2005

10 9 8 7 6 5 4 3 2 1

Printed in the United States of America

CHAPTER 1

The number of people who can do us good is very
small; but almost anyone can do us harm.
—Baltasar Gracian, *The Art of Worldly Wisdom*

"Damn, look at that car, it's flying." Jimmy Arthur
gripped the steering wheel of his Dodge Ram work
van as he looked into his rearview mirror.

Stan Philpot, who was reading the sports section of
the *Orlando Sentinel,* looked up, then ducked back
behind the pages. The national news of late had
been dominated by politics. Democratic presidential candidate Al Gore was keeping the country guess-
ing the identity of his vice presidential running mate.
The first Atlantic hurricane of the 2000 season, Al-
berto, had formed and was strengthening, but it was
the sports section that held his interest. The Florida
Marlins were in third place in the National League
East play-offs and were preparing tonight to play the
St. Louis Cardinals, Central Division leaders. Adrienne
Johnson, of the Orlando Miracles, scored a career-
high 25 points on Sunday, winning over the Detroit

Shock, making way for a WNBA play-off berth for the Miracles.

Arthur had just turned onto Lake Mary Boulevard, off Heathrow Boulevard, and was traveling west. He flipped on his turn signal and was easing into the next lane. He knew from experience the right lane would soon become a turn-only lane. The black BMW had not been visible to him when he had pulled out; suddenly it was there.

Today had been a short workday for the two men. They had spent the day in the community of Heathrow, remodeling a bathroom with ceramic tile. It was around 4:00 P.M. and they were working their way back home to Apopka. The van rocked as the car tore past, almost sideswiping it. The speeding car hadn't been in sight when Arthur had turned onto the main thoroughfare running through the town of Lake Mary, so he knew it was going fast.

Lake Mary is like many other central Florida towns. It flourishes amid the hills and valleys created by the collapse of limestone covering the aquifer. This gave way to lakes—large and small—that dot the countryside or gives way to gentle rolling hills—not hills according to most standards, but in Florida, they are hills. Lake Mary, the "City of Lakes," has many freshwater lakes, popular for all types of recreation. The shorelines are much sought-after sites for waterfront homes. It's a prosperous community, with strip malls and, here and there, a sprinkling of large stand-alone stores—now becoming popular again. Plus, there were myriad service businesses to supply the locals (and tourists) with their daily needs and wants. If more exotic or diverse needs arise, the interstate connects the community to Orlando—the sleepy little town that became a megalopolis—thanks to a mouse and is now one of the most popular tourist destinations in the world. As in most of Florida, old money, new money and little or no money—all live in close proximity, shopping in many of the same stores, using the same community amenities, traveling the same roads.

The "little or no money" folks mostly live in pleasant, small communities in this area. Some, especially retirees, may live in neat, clean mobile-home parks, or they cling to their "cracker-style" homes, once prevalent in this former agricultural area. (An oddity is that many well-to-do people are building expensive new homes, and even businesses, embracing the same old-fashioned Florida construction details and appearances.) Industrial and high-tech areas butt up against residential areas. Schools are plopped down in the midst of seas of homes. Students attending public schools come from all manner of social and economic backgrounds. They study, play, eat and ride school buses together, interacting with each other throughout the school year, although their lives away from school may be very different. It becomes a major equalizer among young people; economic privilege or lack thereof becomes unimportant.

The wealthier residents frequently choose to live behind walls, a guard at the entrance to keep out anyone who doesn't belong. Markham Woods Road has a number of these gated communities, where if you have enough money, you can hope to shut the rest of the world out after you pass the gate guard. It doesn't always work that way, though. Wingfield North is one such community. The tragedy that visited itself on this protected enclave did not come from outside the walls. It had been lurking, festering, growing for years, within their own sprawling community. . . . They didn't lock it out, it was locked in.

Lake Mary Boulevard is a wide ribbon of gray, connecting numerous bedroom communities that lie between and around Lake Mary with Longwood, to the south, Sanford, to the north, and the "main drag" of US 17-92, to the east, connecting it to other communities. Just before approaching the community of Heathrow, the many lanes of the road rise high above I-4. The interstate is always packed with traffic, rushing to or from Orlando, and to points beyond. Not only is it a major thoroughfare for commerce and long-distance travelers, it has become a convenient beltway for residents commuting to jobs and shopping. Local drivers think nothing of shooting into a small opening in traffic, racing down the interstate, caught up in the high-speed traffic, keeping up with the traffic flow. They may "jump off" at an exit a few miles up or down the way—congratulating themselves on having avoided all the traffic lights, stop signs and two-lane streets that comprise the asphalt network connecting the nearby suburban sprawl. It also makes a huge time difference in getting somewhere, traveling seventy to eighty miles per hour instead of twenty-five to forty. Speed gets you there; sometimes it doesn't.

The black car—a large, full-size BMW—shot by Arthur's van, "almost nailing him," he would later recall. Arthur had moved over into the middle lane of the boulevard, anticipating a turn he would navigate at the intersection with Markham Woods Road. He quickly swerved over to avoid the BMW as it continued past him. The BMW was now in the "fast lane," also approaching the intersection, the lane that would become a left-turn lane.

Philpot looked up from the *Sentinel* as they pulled up

to the intersection, behind the BMW. They both could now see down into the car ahead of them. Three young people were in the backseat of the car, two girls and a boy.

"Why is she so white?" Philpot asked, observing the driver.

"I don't know," Arthur replied, "maybe she's ill or something is wrong."

The traffic signal had turned red before the BMW arrived at the intersection. The car slid into the intersection, almost underneath the traffic light. The driver put the car in reverse, backed up about fifteen feet, "burning the tires, making the tires squeal."

Arthur tensed as it appeared that the vehicle that seconds before had almost sideswiped his van was now going to hit the front of his vehicle. *Wow,* he thought.

When the driver brought the car to a stop, just short of his bumper, he noticed the young boy looking up at him, as though to say, "What do I do?" He appeared frightened. He silently advised the boy: "If it was me, I'd get out of there." He could see the driver's reflection in her sideview mirror: she was glaring at him.

Philpot, watching from the passenger seat, was aware of the car in front of them, "inching up," until it was almost back into the intersection as they all waited for the light to change.

The traffic signal turned green and the driver of the BMW took off "fast, real fast."

Although Arthur's and Philpot's recollections of these events are similar in most details, Mary Hill denies their allegations that she was driving fast on Lake Mary Boulevard and that she overshot the intersection and was inching forward into it while waiting for the signal to go green.

* * *

As Arthur and Philpot waited at the intersection
for the traffic signal to change, software engineer Earl
Hodil was waiting on the other side of the intersection
for the signal to change as well. He was bicycling to the
Seminole Ford dealership to pick up his vehicle. He
had approached the intersection from the sidewalk running parallel to Markham Woods Road. It was a relief
to get off the asphalt roadway and onto the sidewalk
where it began in front of the golf course at Alaqua
Lakes. While he was standing astride his bicycle, in front
of the Alaqua Lakes subdivision, the BMW moved past
him as the light changed. He could tell from the
engine noise that it was "accelerating heavily."

While the three men were waiting at the intersection, Debra Zoe Bejerkestrand and her nine-year-
old daughter were walking down the driveway toward
their horse stable. Their home and riding stable were
nestled among trees, bordered by a white fence at the
corner of Lake Mary Boulevard and Markham Woods
Road. On this clear, warm August day, they were
going down to the stable, as was their daily habit, between 4:00 and 4:30 P.M. Although she was 450 to 500
feet from Markham Woods Road, Bejerkestrand could
hear the sound of a car engine. "An engine of a car
that started out as a very deep, low rumble," she described, "and as it . . . as time went on, it became
louder, higher pitched, like a squeal or a whistle."

As the driver of the BMW "gunned it" and sped
down the serpentine, two-lane country road, Arthur

proceeded through the intersection in the same direction. The BMW was probably twenty to twenty-five car lengths ahead of them when the men saw it fishtailing, crossing the yellow line down the middle of the road. "They gonna lose it, Jimmy, they gonna lose it," Philpot said as the men watched the car careen out of control. It was 4:15 P.M. by Arthur's watch.

As they watched helplessly, the car in front of them slid to the left, then jerked back to the right, as it appeared the driver overcorrected the slide. The car rotated and slammed into an oak tree next to the sidewalk Earl Hodil had ridden down, only minutes before. The BMW hit the tree on the left passenger side compartment, just behind the driver's seat, causing the back window to explode out onto the roadway. As they watched helplessly from the van, the car rolled around the tree, ejecting a woman through the open driver's-side window.

Arthur quickly pulled the white van over onto the grassy shoulder of the road. Both men jumped out and ran up toward the now badly mangled BMW, which appeared to be crushed into two distinct pieces. The car looked like a giant had placed his foot in the center of it, squashing it flat, leaving the front and rear bulging out; steam or smoke was pouring from the wreckage, maybe both.

Finally getting a green light, Hodil was now riding across the intersection and was proceeding on his way to the auto dealership. He heard a loud bang behind him. His first thought was that someone at the intersection had rear-ended a vehicle coming out of the nearby subdivision. He turned back to look, but seeing nothing, pedaled on.

About five seconds after hearing the loud engine noises, Bejerkestrand heard tires squealing, then heard a crash, the sound of metal, and still the sound of the engine could be heard, progressing to a loud squeal.

The woman who had been ejected from the BMW was lying partially on the shoulder of the road and the roadway.

The woman tried to get up, but couldn't. She began to crawl toward the smoking car, finally reaching the sidewalk. She told Arthur and Philpot that she "had some kids. Her kids were in the car and to check them and get them out."

It was apparent to Philpot she was injured. She was holding her chest and talking with a slur, but he didn't see any blood.

Quickly turning their attention to the car, Arthur raced to the right side and Philpot to the left. Arthur yanked on the rear passenger door, trying to get it open. Meanwhile, the car engine continued to run and gas was everywhere. "This thing is going to catch on fire," Philpot said. "Turn it off." Reaching inside the driver's compartment, he turned the ignition off himself as Arthur continued to try to open the jammed door. After looking back into the passenger compartment and seeing the children there, he told Arthur, "I can't handle this," and walked away from the crashed vehicle. He didn't go back to it, although the two men were detained there for hours.

At this point, Arthur finally was able to get the door open and looked inside. Reaching across both the boy and the girl in the center of the seat, he felt the neck of the girl who was seated behind the driver's seat. He felt no pulse. Observing the angle of the neck of the girl in the middle, he decided to check for a heartbeat instead of a pulse. Placing two fingers above her heart, he felt a slight heartbeat. The boy was convulsing. The passengers had been so compressed together, the seat belt was pulled too tight for him to get it loose or unbuckled from around the boy.

Standing up, he looked around and saw a man who had just ridden up on his bicycle. He had a cell phone. Arthur asked him to call 911. When the man made the call and reported a single car accident, Arthur asked him to call the dispatcher again and tell them it was serious. After the second call, it was five minutes or less before Arthur heard the approaching sirens.

While they were waiting for the arrival of the emergency crews, Arthur reached into the car and again checked the heartbeat of the girl next to the boy— it had stopped.

Hodil, who was traveling down Lake Mary Boulevard, heard the ambulance sirens as well. Concerned his wife might think he had been in an accident, he called her on his cell phone to let her know he was okay.

A man drove up to the scene as the three men were waiting for emergency crews and law enforcement to arrive. He parked the white Cadillac he was driving on the roadside, as did Arthur with his van. The men watched as he walked over to the injured woman. "What the fuck have you done now? What the fuck have you done again?" Both Arthur and Philpot overheard him demanding this of her.

He continued to talk to her, and Philpot could tell he was scolding her, although they were talking so low now that he couldn't understand what they were saying.

The man walked over to the car and began crying. "Oh, my children; oh, my children." Bending down, he touched the girl on the driver's side, then looked at Arthur. "How do you tell a ten-year-old daughter that her mother just killed her sister?" he demanded.

Arthur asked the man if he would like for him to

pray with him, but the man said, "No," and just walked away, back over to the injured woman.

The man, who made the 911 phone calls at Arthur's request, quietly rode away on his bicycle as the scene began to fill with rescue vehicles and crews, Florida Highway Patrol (FHP) troopers and other law enforcement officers. No one learned his name. He remained a nameless Good Samaritan with a cell phone until much later.

Eventually helicopters came to remove the injured woman and boy to Orlando Regional Medical Center (ORMC). It would be approximately 8:30 P.M. before Arthur and Philpot left the scene, back on their way home to Apopka, a journey they began $4\frac{1}{2}$ hours ago. The sun had set twenty minutes ago, as the men set off in the darkness, down the road. It would take them only a few minutes to pass Wingfield North, the exclusive community that knew nothing of them, but had unknowingly been touched by their efforts. It was a community that would never be the same again.

CHAPTER 2

What greater grief can there be for mortals
than to see their children dead?
—Euripides, *The Suppliant Women*

In the jargon of preliminary accident reports, the result of the car crash on August 7, 2000, was two traffic fatalities and two injuries. It's a simple, unemotional explanation for something that doubtlessly has the most emotional impact to be faced in a lifetime by a parent. Dealing with the grief and fear caused by the death or traumatic injury of your child is the polar opposite of the pure joy and elation over that child's birth. Popular wisdom proposes: "A parent is not meant to outlive his child."

The young girl whom Jimmy Arthur first determined to be dead, when he and Stan Philpot tried to help at the crash scene, was Amanda "Amy" Jordan Hill, thirteen, the daughter of the driver, Mary L. Hill, forty-nine, president of Barbara Nolan Market Research, Maitland, Florida. The angry, grief-stricken man at the scene was the child's father, wealthy marketing executive Dennis G. Hill, CEO of the company and also of U.S. Research Company. His marketing offices dotted across the country, claim such nationally recognized clients as Coca-Cola, the St. Louis Cardinals, Federal Express, Colgate, Ford, Exxon and Nabisco, to name a few.

The other fatality was Carrie Anne Brown, fourteen, daughter of internationally known gymnastic trainer and writer Rita Brown and her ex-husband, Kevin Brown, of Minnesota. Loved ones also left to grieve were older sister Jennifer Brown, who now lives in Los Angeles and works in television, and Mel Stevens Jr., Rita Brown's longtime companion/business associate. He had been Jennifer and Carrie's father figure for many years. Also left to mourn was the family pet Astro, a pug that had known the love of Carrie his whole life. He appeared in some well-known and very publicized photos of Carrie, one that also included Amy.

Both Rita Brown and Mel Stevens have strong, take-charge personalities. Rita has the athletic build of a longtime athlete, but still is very feminine, with her long, blond-streaked hair and tailored yet feminine style of dress. She has a compassionate nature that shows through even heartbreaking tragedy. Her longtime friend Mel Stevens dwarfs her average height, at more than six feet tall. He has dark hair and eyes, with chiseled features. On first impression, you perceive a man in a well-tailored business suit, coiled like a spring, ready for action.

Retired businessman Keith Rockwell, whose thirteen-year-old son Zak Rockwell was left in a coma as a result of crash injuries, received a thrust of the proverbial double-edged sword: his son was alive, although his recovery and the impact of closed-brain injuries were unknown. With the exception of a black eye and some abrasions from the seat belt, Zak appeared to be sleeping when Rockwell first saw him at the ORMC emergency ward immediately after the crash.

Keith Rockwell can best be described as low-key. In another age, he would fit the mold of the well-mannered country gentleman . . . aristocratic, yet reachable and likable. Although his and Zak's lives have been tumultuous after the crash, and his brown eyes often seem weary and sad as they are dragged through court hearing after court hearing, he still has a friendly, ready smile—the same smile as Zak. Zak, who now has matched his dad's tall height, at least six feet or more, has sun-bleached blond hair with a "surfer" cut. At most court proceedings, he was well-dressed in suits or blazer jackets, with open-neck dress shirts. It was only during the hearings for a new trial for Mary Hill when he came to court, directly after school, dressed in casual school attire. The best description of the Rockwells is athletic, low-key and unpretentious.

All three families were residents of the upscale, gated community of Wingfield North, located a few blocks from the site of the crash, on Markham Woods Road. Although the Hills were not personally well-known to Rita Brown, Mel Stevens or Keith Rockwell, they all knew some details about the Hills through their children's friendship with Amy and Kaitlynn Hill. At some time, they all had limited social contact with them. None of them had any idea that the on-going problems of Mary Hill and the Hill family would impact their families in such a tragic manner. The three children were great friends and always seemed to be together. The end of the first day of school in Seminole County was no different. Rita Brown and Keith Rockwell were expecting their children to ride home on the school bus from the Lake Mary middle school all three 8th graders attended. Even when they both heard about a bad accident on Markham Woods Road, it did not occur to either of them that their children were involved.

Seminole County Sheriff's Office (SCSO) deputies were dispatched to the homes of the Browns and Rockwells to notify the families of the crash. In a deposition, Dennis Hill said he actually was the one that told the deputies where the Browns and Rockwells lived. Regardless of how they found their homes, the sad task of family notification began for SCSO deputies. Jennifer Brown, home from college, was given the news.

Jennifer Brown and her friend Jason Agan were at the Brown residence preparing to go for a swim. She was getting ready to bring Astro, the pug, inside the house when she became aware of a man standing outside the front door. She could see him through the etched-glass door before she heard the doorbell ring.

When Jennifer answered the door, she was confronted by a SCSO deputy. "Is Rita Brown here?" he asked.

"No, but I'm her daughter Jennifer."

"How old are you?" he inquired.

"Nineteen," she said, affirming that her age made her an adult, and he agreed.

"There has been a car accident and your sister, Carrie, and he agreed.

"Oh no, you must be mistaken," Jennifer reassured him. "Carrie's coming home on the school bus."

The deputy looked at his hand. He had used it as an emergency notepad, writing notes on it. "Do you know a Dennis Hill?"

Jennifer was beginning to experience the first signs of uneasiness. "Yes," she said.

"Mary Hill and Amy Hill," he inquired.

Jennifer was trying hard to maintain her composure; after all, she was the big sister. Wasn't she supposed to be there for her little sister? "What about Carrie?" she asked.

"She didn't make it."

The voice of the deputy seemed to be coming from a distance as she tried to comprehend what he had just said. Jason was there at her side for support. She could feel the fear and pain welling up in her. "What?"

"Could Mr. Hill identify Carrie?" he asked.

"Yes," she said, knowing she was close to "losing it."

"Where's your mother?" The deputy had to repeat his question.

"At work," she said, her mind swirling, wanting to reject the information that was just delivered. *This couldn't be true,* it was telling her. *Not Carrie. She is on the bus. It has to be a mistake.*

She knew it wasn't a mistake, not if Amy was in the car. It must be true.

"Do you know when she will be home?" the deputy prodded for information.

"No," Jennifer said, trying to remain calm with difficulty. "Her hours vary. She might not be through until nine o'clock, depending upon training sessions."

Just then, the telephone rang. Jennifer ran and looked at the caller ID. "It's Mom," she said to the deputy. "What should I do?"

"Don't answer it," he said firmly.

They could hear the other house phone ringing as Rita tried to reach the girls. (They would later listen to the message she had left. "It's Mom," Rita Brown said, "just checking to make sure Carrie made it home from school safely. I heard there was a bad accident on Markham Woods Road. I want to hear all about the first day of school. Love you. Call me.")

Jennifer tried to decide what to do about letting her mother know what had happened. The officer said that she shouldn't call her, because statistics show that people rushing to get home after a tragedy get into accidents themselves. She couldn't call her on the cell phone, not with this.

She had Jason call Mel Stevens, a real estate broker/developer and mortgage broker, at work. As Jason was trying to tell him what happened, she took the phone from him and blurted out the news. On the other end of the phone line, Stevens was in shock, trying to make sense of what he had just heard. Bracing himself for what he must do, all he could manage to say was, "I'll be right there."

He immediately canceled his pending business meetings so he could rush to Rita Brown's side. "I had to tell my mother that my father had died a few years ago. That was hard. He was the only person who ever stood up for me in my whole life. But to tell the woman you love that the child you both love is dead, [this] is the hardest thing I've ever had to do," he said.

Later, a female victim's advocate from Seminole County would come to the house to talk to them, but by that time, Mel Stevens was on his way to meet Rita.

Brown had left her Altamonte gym to take a laptop computer to a Winter Park repair shop. Stevens called her on her cell phone and told her to wait there, he was coming to her.

"What's wrong?" she wanted to know. But Stevens just told her to wait there.

She met him outside the store as he was getting out

of his car. She sensed something was terribly wrong. "Who?" was all she asked.

"Carrie," he said.

When she asked him how bad, he had difficulty saying the words, "She's gone." Brown collapsed in his arms.

"Not my baby. Not my baby" was all she could say over and over again.

In spite of her grief, Brown contributed Carrie's corneas and heart valves for transplant—her *only* salvageable organs after the high-speed crash.

The SCSO deputies who came to Keith Rockwell's door asked him if he had heard about the accident on Markham Woods. "I heard something about it on the TV," he told them. "I wasn't paying much attention." A single father, raising a teenage son, he was already in the kitchen beginning preparations for the evening meal. The television, turned on in the living area, could be heard, but the sound was faint. "They told me to go immediately to ORMC. I went, not knowing what to expect.

"When I arrived at ORMC, I went to the receptionist's desk in the emergency room. When I told her my name, a man came up behind me and introduced himself as the hospital chaplain. He must have read [the fear in] my eyes, because he said, 'No, no, he's alive. I'm just here to act as hospital liaison. I am going to take you to him and introduce the nurses and doctors to you.'

"It was so strange. We walked into a room divided by curtains. On one side of the curtain was Mary Hill. Zak was on the other side. He looked so perfect, hardly a mark on him, except on his neck from the seat belt and the black eye. He looked like he was asleep. A doctor came in and told me he was in a coma and they were going to transfer him to Arnold Palmer Hospital for Children and Women, which was next door. I walked over to it while they were moving him.

"I had tried to call my ex-wife, Mary, but couldn't reach her. Finally a friend contacted her and told her about the crash. She rushed over to Orlando from her New Smyrna Beach home." The two people who loved him most kept vigil over the comatose boy. They were soon to be joined by many friends, youth and adult, who came to the hospital as they heard about Zak.

The Arnold Palmer medical staff kept a close watch on Zak, who remained in a coma for $3\frac{1}{2}$ days. A neurosurgeon told Rockwell that he had never seen anything like this: for the other passengers to be so traumatized, to be killed, and for another passenger, with them, to escape basically unscathed.

"Zak had three bruises on his brain, two small ones, that the doctors weren't worried all that much about, and a larger one, they were watching closely. Swelling was one of the primary concerns." Rockwell said the support of both his and Zak's friends is what helped him get through the ordeal. "All I—we—could do was just wait. When one of Zak's friends handed him a teddy bear, Zak just woke, said 'Thank you' and sat up.

"It was so normal," Rockwell said. "It was just as someone would be if they woke from sleeping. You would think coming out of a coma would be progressive, like fluttering your eyelids, or moving your hands, but he just sat up, like nothing had happened. Of course, nurses and doctors came running."

It was determined that Zak had suffered some deleterious effects from the crash: some short-term memory loss (he remembers nothing of the actual crash and little shortly beforehand) and a drop of fifteen points in IQ. Lots of tutoring and hard work on his part have brought him back onto the honor roll in his senior year at Lake Mary High School.

CHAPTER 3

Despair exaggerates not only our
misery but also our weakness.
— Luc de Vauvanargues, *Reflexions*

Mary and Dennis Hill seemingly lived a fairy-tale existence in a luxury home, in Wingfield North. The development is a beautiful, well-cared-for, exclusive enclave between Lake Mary and Longwood, Florida.

Unfortunately for them, and for many others around them, their fairy-tale was more like the "Fractured Fairy Tales" by A. J. Jacobs. Those tales still have a "cultlike" following, but are best known as a segment of *The Adventures of Rocky & Bullwinkle Show*, which aired 1959 to 1961 on television. This occurred nearly a decade before the Hills would begin a liaison in the 1970s—which eventually resulted in their marriage in 1983. The point of the "fractured" tales was that all did not end well, and the getting to that end was unfortunate, too.

The Hills' seven-thousand-square-foot brick house at the end of a cul-de-sac claimed amenities most people only dream of: a large pool with guest house, tennis court, putting green and spacious grounds, all surrounded by an imposing, wrought-iron fence.

The house, with charming country-French-style design, gave the appearance from the street of brick solidarity, something the family didn't possess. The glistening white pillars that flanked the front entrance seemed to beckon visitors to the home, promising a gracious, hospitable reception to all who came there. . . . Of course, the Hills didn't build or design the house with those features of such promise, they simply purchased it.

The somewhat modern-designed wrought-iron fence's austerity was softened by the use of substantial brick pillars, which also flanked the driveway. Ribbons of horizontal bands of red brickwork broke up the enormous gray driveway that curved around to the east side of the house, where the garage entrance was hidden from street view. The driveway brickwork, a darker, more solid red brick than the house brick, seemed to be an addition to the hardscape, constructed separately from the time of the house construction.

The piece of property was huge—supposedly, the largest in the development—located at the end of a cul-de-sac for privacy. The property may have played host to a number of recreational amenities, but it gave short shrift to landscaping. Compared to the well-manicured, well-designed, luxurious landscapes of neighboring properties, the Hills' landscape efforts, to put it kindly, were found lacking.

The interior of the home was as spacious as the exterior promised it would be. Indeed, the open design of the downstairs living area did not look cramped, even with the presence of two ebony-finished grand pianos. The furnishings and art objects, obviously expensive, seemed just a little "off" in presenting a cohesive interior design. The mismatched styles and wood finishes of the furniture looked as though they had been purchased haphazardly, on whim, rather than with a total design in mind. Expensive, yes. It just didn't work together, like so many things in the Hills' lives.

The house was only an indication of their lifestyle. They enjoyed a lifestyle that included a choice of luxury cars, many "stabled" at the business office. There were plenty of designer clothes, shoes, other accessories and very expensive jewelry. They owned multiple beach condos that allowed them dwellings on both coasts of Florida. The Anheuser-Busch estate was part of their prestigious properties in Florida, but there were also out-of-state properties—including a farm. Travel was not a problem with two airplanes and a boat. They employed a succession of nannies for their two children. They could literally have anything money could buy. But their fairy-tale life didn't bear close scrutiny. The Hill household was a troubled household—with troubles that were deeply divisive within the family. It didn't take much "scratching" to get below the thin veneer of familial bliss, which they so adroitly portrayed in their little tale, to those on the "outside." Occasionally one of the players would forget a line or throw a tantrum, and then give outsiders a true glimpse of what went on inside the household.

Actually, employees at Barbara Nolan were often the subject of, or witness to, many of Mary Hill's tantrums and could hear the Hills arguing loudly behind the closed door of one or the other of their offices. Both Pat Key and Willis Towne confirmed that Mary Hill was an abusive employer, who routinely humiliated employees in front of others, screaming at them, demeaning them, all the while using very strong language.

They both laugh at the image of the soft-spoken, demure woman depicted on a nationally televised newsmagazine, *48 Hours*. The episode, "Driven To Extremes," featured the Mary Hill case. They were skeptical of her courtroom image as well. "She was a cruel taskmistress," said Key.

"Working with her was very demanding," Towne said, "although at times, she could be very nice. You just never knew what she would be like. One minute, she would have you downstairs at a picnic table, while she was smoking a cigarette, treating you like an equal. She would be telling you about her personal problems or giving you perks, like extra breaks; next thing you knew, she would be screaming at you in front of everyone else, telling you you're—I'm not going to say the word—'an expletive' moron. She was like a Jeykll and Hyde personality."

Key claimed if Hill could have been preceded by a drummer and with someone cracking a whip at the employees as she walked around the office, she would have. At the center of employees Marge Burns's, Towne's and Key's discontent was not only the unprofessional, degrading treatment of employees, but how they were compensated. Pay was also the point of contention for a former nanny, whose depositions and trial testimony were damning to Mary Hill in both civil suits arising from the crash and her trial for vehicular homicide and manslaughter. "They lived in that big house in Wingfield North, had all those fancy cars and designer clothes, on the backs of the employees," said Key. "One thing they did was cut everyone to part time, so they didn't have to pay benefits. Top pay was a little over six dollars an hour, and if you were able to get thirty hours a week, you were lucky."

"At one time I was on salary and worked sixty to seventy hours a week, seven days a week," said Towne.

"I didn't find this out until I quit and went to another marketing company," Key said, "but clients pay extra-per-employee for surveys taken for them on weekends. None of that money was ever passed on to Barbara Nolan employees; we didn't even know about it. And there was no option for not working on Saturday. That was understood. You worked. No extra pay, though."

"I think," said Towne, "the basis of Mary Hill's problems was that she was unhappy. When Dennis Hill was out of town, she was miserable." He was out of town a lot, overseeing his far-flung business sites and spending time with his married mistress and their illegitimate child in Illinois. Dennis Hill's relationship with the woman and the existence of the little boy made Mary Hill very, very unhappy. And when Mary Hill was unhappy, everyone was guaranteed to be unhappy, especially if you worked for her . . . especially if you were her family.

The chain-smoking Mary Hill, unhappy and depressed, soothed her troubled psyche with alcohol and drugs, abusing both prescription and recreational drugs, and becoming party to a long history of domestic violence. The SCSO frequently answered calls to various Hill residences. The Hills may have progressively moved up to more exclusive neighborhoods and more luxurious homes, but their problems seemed to remain the same. There was always domestic violence present in their household, regardless of the caliber of the neighborhood, according to sheriff's office reports.

According to eyewitness accounts, cocaine was the recreational drug of choice. In a nationally televised interview, Mary Hill brushed aside the cocaine allegation, as if there were nothing wrong with it, explaining it away as something she had tried only once. "I have tried it. I won't say I haven't tried it. I don't think trying it once makes you an addict," she told the CBS interviewer Peter Van Sant.

Pat Key said, "I was laughing when I heard Mary Hill make those statements. Mary Hill loved cocaine. She loved coke. In fact, supervisors at Barbara Nolan were preparing to fire some guy working in the phone room, because he was so bad at it. One day, Mary Hill was rushing around, getting ready to leave, saying she 'had to go'. She needed 'to buy something.' This guy took a chance and stepped out of a cubicle and flat out asked her if she was looking for coke. She said, 'Yeah,' and he said he could get her all she wanted. That guy's job was secure. No one could fire him after that. He was her supplier until he finally quit working for Barbara Nolan. Just once? I don't think so."

Towne also knew about the drug dealer. "You don't think stuff like this really happens. It's like stuff TV movies are made of."

The Hills could have had it all: power, wealth, respect and happiness, but somewhere along the way, bitterness and recrimination, fueled by alcohol, drugs and mental-health issues, destroyed their mutual respect and love, and it destroyed their happiness. Unfortunately, that unhappiness visited itself on their own family and their neighbors, usually when Mary Hill was behind the steering wheel of her powerful car.

Mary Hill was earning a reputation for reckless driving, tearing down her long, curving driveway and through the placid neighborhood. She seemed to be an accident waiting to happen. She frequently bragged to employees at Barbara Nolan about how fast she drove. She would gleefully tell them she could make it from the Maitland office to Daytona Beach in less than forty-five minutes. "You know how many stoplights are between that office and I-4," asked former Nolan employee Key, "that's before you even get onto I-4 to start to Daytona Beach. She loved to drive fast. She was very proud of the fact that she drove very fast and drove very aggressively." Key estimated that driving at legal speed limits, it would take a driver at least double that to make the trip. Key recalled Hill regaling the staff with tales of how quickly she could drive from her Maitland office to an Oviedo mall location her company maintained. "She would tell us she could, and she did, make it there in fifteen minutes. Anyone else, it would take at least forty to forty-five minutes' driving time.

"Sure, she would be stopped sometimes, but she had radar detectors, and would buy or flirt her way out of a ticket," said Key, "or managed to luck out—until *that* day. She could flirt her way out of a stop. She was a beautiful, well-put-together woman. She didn't change in appearance until after the accident.

"And, the whole thing about the car with the cruise [control], we all knew the car. When it needed repairs, they would take it themselves [to the dealership] or the gofer would take it over, pick it up and stuff. They had a lot of cars. They were all kept in the parking lot at the Maitland office.

"Dennis was gone all the time, and Mary—no one knew where Mary was a lot of the time," according to Key. "The word around the office was 'Oh, Mary's sick. Or Mary's not feeling good.' The clients would probably have been surprised to know that a twenty-something-year-old girl, Doris Scott, with no marketing or management experience, was running the whole company in Mary's absence. Doris was very loyal to Mary and did a good job," said Key, but still it was a shocking and unsettling situation to other employees. "She ran that company," Key said. "Here you have a multimillion-dollar company, and the business is being run by a girl barely out of her twenties." But eventually even she had enough of Mary Hill, as did some other key employees and, in rapid succession, "we bailed. We were the people she counted on, who bailed on her because [we] couldn't stand being around her anymore. She was so filled with rage. The more people had to deal with Mary, the quicker they ended up leaving. Shortly before the crash, Mary Hill suddenly found herself at the helm of a business, without the employees she had depended upon to get the job done, whether or not she was there. When Doris left, she didn't just leave Mary to run her own company, she left with many of Mary's clients as well, accepting a position with another marketing company."

Key had the occasion to speak to remaining Barbara Nolan employees after the crash. They said the whole demeanor of the office had changed. The nice three-story building, with the marketing office located on the second floor, was in shambles. Employees had to bring their own toilet paper with them to work. The stairwell was filled with trash and the office was no longer bright and clean as it once was. "The whole place has fallen into disarray because Dennis is too busy doing other stuff now."

Another change was that Dennis Hill forbade employees to speak of the crash, in the office, outside the office, between themselves or to anyone else. If they did, they would be immediately fired.

"I do know he has put it (Barbara Nolan) up for sale a couple of times, but the price he's asking is too much. There's a guy I know who would call Willis Towne at the new marketing job, and say he would buy Barbara Nolan if Willis would come run it for him. Willis kept saying, 'No, I can't go back there, even if you would run it. There are just too many memories.' So, it didn't get sold. They are cash strapped [since the crash].

"She had it all, literally wrecked it. It's truly a case of how the mighty have fallen. To live in a house in Wingfield North and have everything at your fingertips with literally enough money to burn—to have so much money you literally didn't know what to do with it, and now she's living in what—a five by seven cell? She really did it. It's gone, all the money they had, it's gone to the attorneys."

CHAPTER 4

To dread no eye, and to suspect no tongue,
is the greatest prerogative of innocence.
—Samuel Johnson, *The Three Ramblers:*
in three volumes

August 7, 2000, was the first day of school for eighth graders Carrie Brown, Amy Hill and Zak Rockwell. All three were friends and neighbors. The day began at Carrie Brown's household like any other first day of school. Her sister, Jennifer, checked on her to make sure she was up and getting ready. Carrie showed her mother, Rita, the outfit she had selected to wear. Rita gave her a hug and reminded her to call after school to tell her what her first day had been like. Brown's work schedule at her gymnastics studios necessarily involved late-afternoon hours of work, as budding gymnasts came in to train after they were out of school. The three neighbors would take the school bus to their first day of school.

Mel Stevens later recalled he had passed by the school about an hour before dismissal time. He has struggled with his anguish. "If I had only known what

I know now, I would have stopped and taken her out of school early."

Rita Brown echoed the same thoughts, her voice choked with tears. "I thought she was taking the bus home. If I had only known, I would have left the studio and gone to pick her up."

Today, Keith Rockwell, his voice heavy with emotion, can only say of his good fortune, "Thank God."

While Brown, Stevens and Rockwell were confident their children were safe in their schoolrooms, getting reacquainted with friends and teachers they had not seen since the end of last school year, Mary Hill was at her Jacana Drive home in Wingfield North, anticipating an afternoon appointment. Her husband, Dennis, had already left for work, but would return to accompany her to the appointment. Her regular psychiatrist, Dr. Jose Suarez, had decided he had taken her as far as he could with conventional drug therapy for her depression. It was a mental condition she had struggled with, along with alcoholism and drug addictions, for a long time. He thought she needed electro-convulsive therapy (ECT), and had referred her to a specialist in ECT, psychiatrist Dr. Eduard Gfeller, whose office was next to Florida Hospital in Sanford.

Dennis Hill did arrive home early in the afternoon to drive his wife to her appointment. According to a deposition, he said he came home no earlier than usual, his normal routine being to end his workday in time to be home around 2:00 or 2:30 P.M.

He decided to drive Mary's black BMW 740iL, a car registered to him, but it was considered her car. Dennis Hill never drove the car, he would testify, preferring his own white Mercedes, which he had driven earlier in the morning. Under oath, he would later say his decision to use it that afternoon was prompted by the fact it was a faster car than his own Mercedes.

He drove Mary to her psychiatric appointment, but later would say he was not present during the doctor's examination and didn't really know what went on in the office. The doctor recalled seeing and speaking to him on their arrival. For Mary Hill, it was good news. Gfeller didn't feel ECT was the appropriate method of treatment at the time, and planned to continue a treatment with the use of drugs.

According to Mary, Amy had asked her earlier to pick her up at school. Mary Hill testified they were a little early, so Dennis drove to a nearby service station and filled the tank with gasoline. Dennis would say later in testimony that he drove directly to the school from the doctor's office. Driving from Sanford to Lake Mary, they arrived at the school before dismissal, parking the car near the library, to wait for Amy.

Amy boarded the school bus to tell Carrie and Zak, who were already on board, to "come on," they had a ride home. All three children got into the BMW driven by Dennis Hill. They piled into the backseat with their book bags, buckling themselves in. It was a little after 3:30 P.M.

Instead of immediately proceeding to Wingfield North, Dennis Hill, instead, drove to an Exxon station (now a Shell station) on International Parkway in Heathrow. He wanted to pick up a vehicle he had left for repair.

As Dennis Hill spoke with David Long, owner of the station and garage, Mary Hill got out of the passenger seat, walked around the front of the car and got behind the wheel of the BMW. She did not buckle the seat belt. At some point in the ride, whether at this point or later, the driver's-side window was rolled

down. While Dennis continued to talk with Long,
Mary Hill pulled out of the station onto International
Parkway, for what was to be a short, final, fatal ride for
two passengers, her own daughter Amy and Amy's best
friend, Carrie.

Under oath, Dennis Hill testified he had found
nothing wrong or unusual in the way the car handled
when he had driven it earlier. He said he noticed nothing unusual in the manner in which Mary left the station, turning onto the busy road. In a conversation
a few days after the crash, with FHP homicide investigator Corporal Phillip C. Wright, who investigated
the crash, Dennis Hill said he thought she was driving
fast when she left the station. It was only a few blocks
up the road to Lake Mary Boulevard, where Mary
would soon interact with Jimmy Arthur's van, and take
the three captive passengers in the backseat on what
was a doomed ride. A ride she would survive, thanks
to the open window and lack of seat belt, with a few
broken ribs, a below-the-knee leg injury and a con-
cussion. Her passengers were not so fortunate.

Mary Hill was not reticent about telling neighbors
of her psychiatrist's diagnosis, whether or not it was
for the "shock" value or a way of garnering their sympathy. Rita Brown was shocked to hear the diagnosis
of Dr. Suarez; all she could say at first was "What?"
when Hill phoned her with the news. After imparting
the news, Mary asked Brown if she thought it would
hurt. Actually, the phone call was doubly unusual in
that Rita Brown had little contact with the Hills.
Today, she still struggles with her feelings about Mary
Hill, saying, "She was a neighbor I knew, primarily as
the mother of Carrie's best friend." The only time the
elder Hills had been in her home was when she had

invited them to a gala Christmas party, after Carrie had begged her to do so.

Another nearby Hill neighbor, Vicki Hartzell, who no longer wanted to discuss anything about Mary Hill, said, "I am sick of the Mary Hill case, and don't want to talk about it or her after all the pain she has caused my family." Hartzell was once disconcerted to find a disoriented Mary Hill wandering unsteadily in her driveway. Not comfortable with the behavior Hill was displaying, Hartzell promptly forbade her children from riding in a vehicle with Hill at the wheel.

In fact, Hill's erratic, reckless driving was the topic of discussion among the Brown family and Stevens as well. Carrie knew she should not ride in the car if Mary Hill was driving—although, in the past, Hill had picked up all the children from school occasionally and brought them home. Stevens and Rockwell and Deane David, a Hill nanny, who had worked for the Hills six months prior to the crash, had done the same.

"I once saw Mary get into a terrible argument with Amy about a promised shopping trip to the mall. She was so angry, she got in her car with Kaitlynn (the Hill's youngest daughter, nine years old at the time) as a passenger. She tore down the drive in her car at a high rate of speed. I was terrified for Kaitlynn," said David.

Hill's use of her car as a method of displaying her anger apparently was known to the extended Hill family and was not a new manifestation or display. Dennis Hill's two older daughters from his first marriage contacted CBS's *48 Hours Investigates*, after learning their father and stepmother were the subject of an upcoming episode. In an interview, they told how they had sat terrified in the backseat of a car driven by Mary Hill as she raced out of control, after becoming angry with their father, at speeds up to ninety miles per hour. "I just thought it was a matter of time before something tragic happened," one daughter told the interviewer. "She was a time bomb waiting to go off."

Mary Hill apparently has always been "at odds" with the children from husband Dennis's first marriage, maintaining they have always resented her.

Since he lived farther back in the development, information about Hill's speeding down her driveway and street, and her reckless disregard for the safety of her children while she was driving, had not yet reached Keith Rockwell. He had no idea there was anything to fear with Mary Hill giving his son a ride. He had yet to learn, but would soon experience firsthand, the tragic result of a ride with the neighborhood "speed demon."

"Why didn't Dennis Hill just take them with him or take them home first?" both Brown and Stevens have asked many times.

"There is no way I would put anyone, especially those children, in a car with someone driving, if I knew they were drug addicted, alcoholic and having mental problems. Why did he do it?" Mel Stevens asked. "He had to know. There's no way, he couldn't have. If he had just taken them home, then got the car later, they would still be alive. I hold him just as responsible as I do Mary Hill for Carrie's and Amy's deaths."

Brown and Stevens combined forces with Florida state legislator Lee Constantine to propose legislation that would hold second parties responsible for endangerment, if they knew another party who committed a felony while driving was incapable or incapacitated and should not be driving. The initiative became known as the "Carrie Brown Law." The idea was similar to an existing Florida law that holds

bartenders (or someone plying the drinks) responsible for allowing someone to drink to the point of in-
toxication, then allowing them to drive drunk and
commit a felony. Constantine would later say,
although he thought the idea was a good one, and
that he understood their grief, other legislative members thought laws in place were sufficient and could
be used for prosecution by the state, if sufficient evidence was available.

CHAPTER 5

One of the most beautiful qualities of true
friendship is to understand and to be understood.
—Seneca

At the time of their deaths, a student at Greenwood
Lakes Middle School remembered Carrie Brown and
Amy Hill as being close to each other. She described
them eating together, riding home together—they
simply seemed to be together always.

All three students, Carrie, Amy and Zak, were popular with both faculty and students alike at their middle
school. In a large school, it's unusual for a principal to
recall individual students, but then-principal Michael
Mizwicki, now working at an Oviedo, Florida school,
still remembers all three children, more than four
years after the fatal crash. "They were exceptional,
talented children," he said. The day after the crash, he
recalled how he had only "seen them yesterday." He
termed it a "very difficult" time, as counselors were
made available at Greenwood Lakes Middle School for
anyone needing to talk to them, to deal with the

tragedy, the day after the crash. At least fifty students did talk to the counselors, some asking to go home.

Greenwood Lakes Middle School is the typical Florida school. It's a sprawling complex in the midst of sprawling neighborhoods. The architecture is nothing spectacular; it's best described as functional. Students within a two-mile limit get to school on their own—by foot, bicycle, skateboard, and infrequently by Rollerblades; or their parents drive them to school. Students outside the two-mile limit are eligible to ride the public school buses. Generally the three eighth graders from Wingfield North rode the bus to and from school. Although the children of privilege, the three were accepted universally by all the students, regardless of the economic realities of their lives. The student body raised money and presented two stone benches to the school in Carrie and Amy's memory.

At the May 23, 2001 dedication of the benches, many students, faculty, families, and friends gathered for a dedication invocation, which in part reads:

"We are called to the purpose of remembering Carrie Brown and Amy Hill with an offering.

"We present these two granite benches, crafted with loving hands to honor our two Greenwood Lakes Middle schoolgirls."

At the dedication, it was recalled how the "girls were special friends and special students and need to be remembered." Because the girls were so well-liked, the students project to make a lasting memorial to them at the school quickly took shape.

A survey of eighth-grade students at Greenwood Lakes Middle School resulted in the decision to place memorial benches at the school in the girls' memory. In a cooperative effort, all the funding came from students and their families. The school's parent-teacher-student association (PTSA) assisted with the project, helping the students to complete the project. As part of the project, they raised money not only for the benches but for surrounding landscaping that PTSA planted for the students.

"Granite was chosen for the benches because of its strength and ability to stand against the elements," the speaker said.

The benches were selected in hopes they would become a meeting place for the students there and for future students, as well. They would have a place to come to, to be quiet and reflect, or just to meet with their friends.

The benches were called a symbol of the day on which they were dedicated, the National Day of Prayer, Meet You at the Flag Pole. It is an annual day where "students break down denominational barriers, coming together to pray for the school."

Students, parents and faculty members gathered for the ceremony at the school were asked to remember Amy and Carrie in the special place they had created in their memories. They were reminded to cherish their own lives and to live each day to the fullest. The beautiful dedication ceremony concluded with a prayer, dedicating the benches to Carrie Brown and Amy Hill. Described as "walking in care and love," the desire was expressed that they always remember the two whose loss had brought the whole community closer together. The prayer concluded with the petition that the benches be a reminder to those there and for "future generations to walk in strength, courage, and peace in a busy world."

A neighborhood pal remembered them in a poem that she gave to Rita Brown as a memorial gift, entitled *Crazy Driver.*

The poem related the young friend's anguish over the deaths of her two friends by a person she called "a crazy driver." Although Mary Hill's name was not mentioned, the intent was obvious—she was fully blaming Hill for taking the girls' lives.

The writer's poetic lament told of her devastation at their loss and the fact that she would never again hear their laughter or jokes, or even see their tears. She said she would miss Amy's love of dancing and Carrie's "heartwarming glow," and she mentioned never being able to attend their weddings, the one thing most young girls begin planning at an early age.

What made these three children so unique? Perhaps their easy camaraderie attracted the attention of other students and their neighborhood friends. Carrie, at fourteen years old, was a year older than Amy and Zak. Victim of a learning disability, she was held back in the fourth grade at Heathrow Elementary School. She repeated that grade, overcame her reading disability and became an honor roll student. Teacher Linda Albury never forgot the bright, cheerful girl who had been her student. She, along with her class at the time of Carrie's death, named a star in the Columba constellation, The Dove, in Carrie's memory. The star was officially registered with the Millennium Chronicle and the star deed was presented to Rita Brown.

Not allowing their good deed to go unrewarded, Brown furnished new computers for the learning-disabled class at Heathrow Elementary. "I wanted to be sure they received new computers," she said. "Usually they get the hand-me-downs."

That actually is not the only good deed performed in Carrie's name. Brown equipped a fitness room at Greenwood Lakes Middle School for the use of students and faculty. A muralist painted exercising figures along the walls. Angel Carrie and her pug dog, Otis, who had died, look down upon the exercisers from a cloud. Across the room, Amy Hill jogs toward them. The Carrie

Brown Foundation, a not-for-profit organization, gives summer scholarships to YMCA Camp Wewa, one of Carrie's favorite places. She was hoping to become a counselor there in the summer of 2001. Today, campers can enjoy the large rock-climbing wall and the rifle and archery ranges that Rita Brown donated. (People wanting to contribute to this good cause can send their tax-deductible donation to: Carrie Brown Foundation, Inc., 740 Orange Avenue, Altamonte Springs, FL 32714. Or you can access the foundation Web site at www.carriebrownfoundation.org for more information about both Carrie and the organization.)

Carrie and Zak were more athletic than Amy. Carrie excelled in archery and riflery at Camp Wewa and was just as good in team sports. She played both soccer and on a coed basketball team, coached by Mel Stevens. Her personal goal was to attend Bishop Moore High School and break the record for varsity letters earned over a four-year period, held by older sister Jennifer Brown (the record still stands).

Zak, more into individual pursuits, enjoyed four-wheeling and surfing. He still pursues those hobbies today, as an honor roll senior at Lake Mary High School. He has moved up from the four-wheel ATV to motocross and dirt bikes. He still surfs at Ponce Inlet, off New Smyrna Beach.

Amy, a straight-A student, excelled not only academically, but was a talented pianist and dancer. She and Carrie formed a special bond, helping each other and giving each other support. Amy would often help Carrie with homework, as would Mel Stevens. Carrie gave Amy the emotional support she needed, considering her family situation, problems she frequently confided to Carrie.

Rita Brown remembered looking up from preparing dinner one night and seeing Amy outside their door crying. She told Rita and Carrie that her parents were fighting again, and asked if she could spend the night with them. Rita never asked for details, assuming it was just an argument between a husband and wife. Amy wrote Carrie a poignant letter, apologizing for her "dysfunctional" family and telling her how much she wished that she, Rita and "Chip" (Mel) were her family, instead. "Your family is awesome," she wrote in another letter. "I know you think my family is psycho."

Despite the problems at home, she is remembered today as a sweet, talented, intelligent girl. The soft brown eyes and ready smile belied the strength within. Although her parents had prepaid her tuition to attend a Florida state university, she apparently often informed her father that she intended to attend Harvard. She wanted to become a doctor.

Whereas Amy was slim and had the delicate build of a dancer, and still seemed childlike in appearance, Carrie was the fit, athletic girl-next-door type. It was only in the last months of her life that Carrie began to turn into the physical beauty that reflected her inner self. She was naturally slimming down and taking on a much more feminine appearance than the childish, athletic one, remembered by her schoolmates from the previous year. Her appearance the first day of school must have been both startling to those who knew her, and satisfying to her.

Not to be outdone by Rita Brown's generosity and community spirit, Dennis and Mary Hill also proposed to create memorials in Amy's name. Dennis Hill was reported by a local newspaper as having established a scholarship in Amy's name, at the Catholic Church of the Nativity, in Longwood, their home parish. Four years after the crash, it took some effort by the church administration to find out what had happened to that scholarship, although they were certain it had been created and was in place. Their phone calls to the former education director, who had moved to another state, came up with the answer. An annual education scholarship of $1,000 was set up in Amy's name, and apparently tuition was supplied for three years for a student. It initially had been set up to be a long-term arrangement, but citing the loss of "a lawsuit," the arrangement ended.

It was reported that other scholarships in Amy's name were established at a Longwood music school and a dance school. Charles Moore, who owns the Sweetwater School of Music, was Amy's piano teacher for two years. He termed her a student with "great potential." The local newspaper article stated a music scholarship had been set up for a deserving music student. Moore would neither confirm nor deny this, saying, "I don't have anything to do with the Mary Hill case. I don't want to be involved. I don't know anything about Mary Hill. I don't know why you would even call me."

Actually, his involvement may be more than he thinks. The beneficiary of Dennis Hill's generosity in the past, it was rumored that the Cadillac that Dennis Hill picked up at the Exxon station on August 7, 2000, was to be a gift to Moore. That decision by Dennis Hill—to stop at the service station to pick up the vehicle—created the situation for Carrie's and Amy's deaths, and Zak's injuries to occur—if indeed, the BMW itself was not at fault. No one would confirm or deny this rumor of the Cadillac gift, including Moore. Even in trial cross-examination, Dennis Hill, when asked about the vehicles he owned, didn't include it in his testimony. When lead state prosecutor Pat Whitaker asked him if he did not include that car, because in his mind he didn't own it any longer, having given it away, his answer was in the affirmative.

Once, when Moore was ill, Dennis Hill, a talented

musician, helped Moore out by giving lessons to his students and keeping the music school open. Moore would not return any phone calls to this book's author, although he had agreed to a phone conversation, naming a day and time to call again. He "would decide by then if he wanted to talk." He apparently decided not to talk, even to the point of saying that in person. Instead of answering the call at the appointed time, he let his answering machine do his talking for him. It didn't say much, but at the same time spoke volumes by not accepting the call.

The other memorial to Amy was to be scholarships at the dance school that Amy and Kaitlynn Hill attended, Rolann's School of Dance, also in Longwood. Rolann Owens, who operates the dance school, would not confirm or deny the existence of the scholarships. In a November 2004 phone conversation, she said she wasn't sure she wanted to answer any more questions about the Hills. It's unclear whether or not the scholarships exist, or ever existed. Preparing to leave the country for a trip to Germany, she said she wasn't sure she could stand by earlier statements she had made. She didn't elaborate on the meaning of that statement or which statements she was referring to. Possibly she was referring to her accounts of Kaitlynn Hill's horrifying ride to the dance studio with her mother, Mary Hill. She simply hung up the phone after saying she would be back in the country after December 5 and to call back then. She accepted no more phone calls.

CHAPTER 6

Love is the beauty of the soul.
                              —Saint Augustine

Amy was drawn to the Brown family, as the many notes and letters she wrote to Carrie revealed. One note, printed in Amy's open, rounded style, was embellished with squiggly drawings, using the girls' own special shorthand. It revealed their close relationship. Their easy camaraderie was apparent, as Amy addressed Carrie with a salutation of "Hey babe!"

The note related details about a trip to Ft. Lauderdale and her plan to call Carrie that night. The trip was apparently a piano or dancing competition, although it didn't make clear which—but she was anticipating long, grueling hours, with the competition beginning at 6:30 A.M. and not ending until 10:30 or 11:00 P.M. Ever thinking about her friend, she remembered that Carrie had made a trip to the mall, wishing that she had fun there. She was anticipating seeing her on Monday. She closed with a drawing of a heart and "always, Amy."

Amy envied the Brown family's loving relationship,

such as the one the Brown sisters enjoyed and the way they and a large circle of friends seemed to always have fun together. In August 2000, Jennifer Brown, Carrie's older sister, had just completed a year of college, followed by two months of study in Spain. It seemed as though she hadn't been home in a long time. She was looking forward to giving everyone the gifts she had brought back for them and to tell them all about Spain. She arrived home from the airport around 4:00 A.M. on Saturday, August 5, 2000, two days before the fatal crash.

If Carrie was the ideal picture of the girl next door, with her freckle-splattered face, tan from outdoor sports and her easy grin, her older sister was the type of glamorous big sister that little girls always envy and look up to. Jennifer, slim yet athletically built, was bronze tanned with long, blond-frosted hair. Very beautiful, she recently was featured in advertisements in major national fashion and health magazines.

Ordinarily, after such a long trip and crossing time zones, a traveler would be experiencing jet lag, but Jennifer woke up early, refreshed by a little sleep, and handed out the gifts. Everyone was happy, laughing and just being a family—all back together again.

Courtney Phillips, Jennifer's best friend since the second grade, came over to visit. They planned on going for manicures and pedicures later in the day. Mel gave Carrie $30 as a treat, so she could accompany them. But later in the day, when the girls were ready to leave, after Mel and Rita had gone for a motorcycle ride, Carrie decided to stay home. She said she wanted to be by herself for a while. No amount of cajoling could convince her to come with them. Carrie and Astro stayed home together, alone.

Later that night, Jennifer was teaching Courtney

some of the salsa moves she had learned in Spain. They even managed to get Carrie, who never danced, to learn some of the salsa dances Jennifer had picked up. All three girls were salsa dancing around the house, just being girls together, just having fun.

After dancing, "Courtney and I just fell on Carrie's bed and started to watch TV with her," Jennifer said. "It was pretty funny, because we were all laying in her bed, with Carrie sandwiched in between us. She kept on asking us to leave and we wouldn't get up. After hanging out for a while, we finally left and let her go to bed."

On Sunday, their last full day together, they were preparing for a clothes shopping trip for Carrie. They had been told about a special discount day at a favorite store. Afterward, they were going to meet at the movie theater to see *Coyote Ugly*. Mel elected not to go; *chick flick*, he decided, so he followed his own pursuits that afternoon. Rita and Carrie would spend the afternoon picking out some great outfits, which Carrie later modeled for everyone, after they returned home that evening.

After the shopping trip, Carrie was standing outside the movie theater, arms folded across her chest, when Jennifer arrived. She held out an admission ticket to her. "You're late," she told her sister. "Mom's mad."

Jennifer just looked at her and asked, "You want to get some Sour Patch Kids?"

Carrie considered for a few seconds; then the characteristic good humor broke forth in a big grin: "Sure."

The girls went in together, to find their mother, who was already inside saving seats for them. At first, they seated themselves with Rita sitting between them, but when Rita came back from a visit to the lobby, Carrie had moved into her seat. No argument could convince her to move back to her original seat. The three spent the remainder of the movie, with Carrie seated between them.

On the morning of the first day of school, Rita phoned Jennifer's room around 7:30 A.M. Their house had a split plan with the master suite being separated by the living area from the other bedrooms. "I always hated it when she did that," Jennifer said. "Sometimes I wouldn't even pick up the phone. But I did for some reason that morning."

"Would you go make sure Carrie's up," Rita asked, "and getting ready for school?"

Jennifer got out of bed and found Carrie's bed empty. She was in the bathroom. "Are you getting ready?" Jennifer asked.

Carrie's muffled voice came through the door, saying she was.

"Have a good day at school," Jennifer told her. The girls had previously planned for Carrie to wear Jennifer's boots and an accessory, with one of the new outfits. It was only after the accident that Jennifer realized Carrie had not worn the boots, but a pair of her own shoes. She had worn nothing to school that day except her own clothing.

Later in the morning, around 11:00 A.M., before Rita had to go to work, Jennifer and her mom were walking around outside with the dog. "I am so thankful to have Carrie for a sister. It is going to be great growing old with her," she told her mom.

Later in the morning after Rita had departed for the gymnastics studio, a longtime friend came over to the house. Jennifer wanted to show her Carrie's recently redecorated room. It looked heavenly, with the border of golden suns, moons and stars wrapping the top of the walls, just below where it touched the ceiling. Their golden glimmer against dark blue heavens would always be there to shine down on Carrie and the shelves containing the Beanie Babies—plush toys that Rita was always giving her as rewards and love tokens. As they were walking out of Carrie's room, Jennifer said, "I am so glad Carrie is going to try to break my record at Bishop Moore. If anyone breaks it, I am glad it is going to be her."

After the news of the tragedy circulated around the community, Courtney Phillips came again to the Browns, to comfort Jennifer and the rest of the family. Her father accompanied her and took phone calls and gathered information to make arrangements, as Rita, Mel and Jennifer tried to make sense of the terrible thing that had befallen their family. Their "bright and shining star" had been taken away, as Stevens would describe her later, when trying to tell how Carrie's death had affected his mother, who considered both Jennifer and Carrie to be her grandchildren.

Carrie's death left many heartbroken grandparents. Her maternal grandparents, Mel and Cecilia Fragassi, reside in Deerfield, Illinois. They were in Sanford at the end of 2004 for the first Hill hearing at the new Seminole County Courthouse, a continuance on the defense's appeal for a new trial. They, too, are still struggling with her loss. Carrie's paternal grandmother, widow Belva Brown, lives in Faribault, Minnesota. She and Carrie shared a birthday party together in July, just before she was to begin the new school year. Her grandfather, Ralph Brown, predeceased her.

After the fatal crash, a tearful Mel Stevens showed Rita $30 he had found on the dresser. It was the $30 he had given Carrie for a manicure. "She didn't have to give it back," he said. But, after all, that was the kind of girl Carrie Brown was.

Carrie had a "thing" that she always did, Rita remembered. She would come up to her mom or to Jennifer and tug at their elbows or sleeves, as if to say, "I'm here, love me."

"We would feel a little tug, and without even looking, we knew it was Carrie."

Jennifer wrote a poem dedicated to Carrie's memory, "Your Memory Will Always Live On." It expressed her love for her sister and her appreciation for the times they shared. It read in part:

> There are so many things that I would give up
> Just to see you one more day.
> As my life goes on I know you will be there
> Telling me it will be okay.
>
> I just wish I could tell you how proud I was
> To have you as a sister all to my own.
> Watching you grow from the tomboy I was.
> Now a young lady, oh how you have grown.
>
> But just when you think they will always be there
> You turn around and then they are gone.
> But as long as you remember the times that you've
> shared,
> Their memory will always live on.

Jennifer and Carrie Brown's home life, and their relationship with each other and their family, was entirely different from the one that Jennifer Wilson shared with sisters Amy and Kaitlynn Hill—and with the rest of the extended Hill household. It was a household of individuals and personalities that never got along with each other. Mary's own three daughters had the best relationship of all with each other, out of a total of seven Hill children. The extended family blended Dennis Hill's three children from his first marriage, another son with his mistress, Mary's daughter from her first marriage and the two children from their own union. The combination formed a classic dysfunctional family that could not, and would not, find a way to get along with each other. Instead of a family of love, it was a family that harbored hatred toward each other. The older Hill children blamed Mary for breaking up their parents' marriage. They hated Mary and her daughter Jennifer, a sentiment Jennifer returned.

Jennifer Wilson has the compact build of an athlete—she is an accomplished horsewoman, with a creamy ivory complexion and very long brown hair. She has a look about her, very much resembling early photographs of her mother, Mary Hill, who was shown by photo-graphs to have been outstandingly beautiful when younger. Jennifer differed in appearance from her sisters Amy and Kaitlynn. Amy, although possessing the same ivory skin tone, had darker eyes and darker brown hair, with a very slim build. Kaitlynn now has long, bright, strawberry-blond hair, dark eyes that can dance with mischief and the light porcelain skin that many redheads possess. She has a dancer's grace and athleticism when she moves.

Jennifer Wilson is Mary Hill's daughter from her failed marriage to a Chicago cop of first-generation French descent. He is now retired from Chicago law enforcement and lives in California. "When he walked out on Mom, he left her with nothing, and I wasn't even two years old," Jennifer said.

Mary had worked for U.S. Research Company, Dennis Hill's marketing firm in Chicago, prior to her husband leaving her. She had left that job for another, then quit that and had became a full-time mother.

When she suddenly found herself in need of a job again, she went back to Hill's firm.

Jennifer remembered how she felt when she was thirteen years old and Amy was born. Dennis and Mary Hill had been married for approximately five years before Amy's birth. Jennifer didn't want a sister. She didn't want to be a baby-sitter. Bitter at her own treatment by her older stepsisters, Julie and Heather, from Dennis's first marriage, she took her anger out on little Amy, by her own admission. "I was mean to her, but it wasn't her fault. I hated her." Later, she tried to make it up to Amy, explaining why she had acted the way she had. It wasn't long before Amy died that they were beginning to have a great relationship. Very much like the one they both had with their younger sister, Kaitlynn.

"When I got older, about eighteen, I realized how wrong I was for hating her. I mean, I really knew I was wrong. She and I talked about this so many times. I would say, 'Amy, I know I was a total bitch. I didn't want the responsibility of having a sister. It was never you.' I just did what I could to make it up to her. When she died, we were really just starting to have a good relationship. I had made a point to really try, you know, to make one with her, because I was always close to Kaitlynn.

"Kaitlynn and I have always been inseparable; she was sort of like me, if you know what I mean. There are sisters who are alike and sisters who are opposite; Amy really wasn't like me.

"Amy was a lot like my (other) stepsisters," Jennifer said. "She was very smart, very articulate. I was more of a tomboy—she was a dancer. I liked my horses. I was very artistic and Kaitlynn is kind of the same way. We're totally opposite of Amy, who kind of took on my stepsisters' looks," with her dark hair and eyes and creamy-colored complexion.

"They made one of my stepsisters her godmother. My stepsisters and I hated each other. Of course, I turned that toward Amy, because I lived with her for a little bit," before beginning college. "I was completely wrong, and I really tried to make it up to her before she died, and I don't know if I did a good enough job, but I guess I will know one day.

"One of the last [memorable] times I saw my sister Amy alive was at my wedding. My husband and I eloped, and our families were pretty mad at each other. You know my family's wealthy, (but) they refused to help us with a dime of the wedding. Mike's parents are not wealthy like my parents, but they are well-off. They own their own business. He's a dairy farmer and very well-known in Canada. So, we had the wedding in Canada. My parents barely showed up in time, and my mom caused a huge scene. My dad (Dennis Hill, whom she always refers to as her father), refused to help out, and he wouldn't let the girls stay. That was one of the last times I saw Amy alive.

"I was the last person to be notified. It was eleven forty-five that night. Everyone else was already on planes to come down here and I hadn't even been told. Dennis picked Kaitlynn up and took her to the hospital."

It must have been a traumatic ride for the young girl. "He told Kaitlynn that Amy and Carrie were dead, that Zak was in a coma and that Mom was in the hospital, on the way over to the hospital; then he leaves her there by herself. She's an eleven-year-old child." After four years, Jennifer's indignation still resonated over his lack of concern for his youngest daughter's welfare that night. "He decides he needs to go get my grandmother or some other people. So, she's stuck at the hospital by herself with my mother, who is out cold. She can't talk, she's not conscious. Kaitlynn was there by herself for a very long time. Things were awful.

"When Amy died, I had to go shopping, because we didn't know what she would want to wear. I said, 'You know what Amy would have really liked? Something new. We'll go buy her something new and put a new dress on her, that's what she would have liked, not something that you grabbed out of her closet.' So, I had to go shopping and had to buy her a new outfit. Kaitlynn went with me and never cried. Nothing."

CHAPTER 7

Three things cannot be long hidden:
the sun, the moon, and the truth.
                                        —Buddha

At the time of the crash, Corporal Phillip C. Wright had been with the FHP for thirty-one years. He has since retired after thirty-three years of service, but still serves as a reserve officer, assisting the homicide squad. He has graying brown hair, with a somewhat receded hairline, parted on the side. He wears gold-framed aviator glasses and walks with an easy lope. In another age, you could easily picture him leaving an investigation, swinging his leg over his horse's saddle, preparing to ride off into the sunset, to fight "bad guys" another day and somewhere else. He has a nice, friendly smile—although at times, he can look very stern. . . . It comes with his territory. The things he sees and the things he investigates are not pretty.

On the day of the crash, he was the second FHP homicide investigator on the scene. Actually, he was the third—if you count crash investigator Corporal Lawrence P. Smith, who, in the past, had been a homicide investigator, but now was working traffic. Smith was the first trooper on the scene. Soon there would be many more people to assist, including highway patrolmen and sheriff's deputies and rescue teams, but Corporal Smith already had begun the careful process of collecting and preserving evidence—working the scene.

Corporal David A. Templeton, also a homicide investigator, was the next highway patrolman on the scene. He was carrying a heavy caseload of investigations at the time. After he and Corporal Wright consulted later at the scene, it was decided Corporal Wright would be the homicide investigator for the case. His current caseload was lighter. Corporal Templeton remained on the scene, taking photographs and interviewing witnesses Jimmy Arthur, Stan Philpot and later Earl Hodil, who came down to the scene on the advice of his wife. In general, Templeton was assisting in conducting the investigation while evidence and witnesses were available.

Most people's perception of the Florida Highway Patrol is of a shiny tan-and-black car parked behind another car while a snappily dressed, uniformed trooper writes out a ticket for some hapless speeder. Only recently could that trooper be a man or a woman. There is more to what troopers do than write speeding tickets, however.

Back in the mid-1960s, it became a specialized appointment to serve as a FHP homicide investigator. "At first, troopers were sent to advanced schools for homicide investigation; then it became a position of promotion. The troopers would have to have a minimum of three years on the road; then they would take a promotional exam," said Sergeant Rick Ritter, head of the

Deland FHP homicide squad, which serves a large segment of the surrounding central Florida area.

"From that point, they go to the academy and [attend] the basic homicide investigators school, which is an eighty-hour [course]. After that, field training is involved, where they learn new technologies and theory. They regularly go back to the academy in Tallahassee, or to some of the other advanced schools, to get specialized training, for instance— pedestrian death, motorcycles, advanced investigations and reconstruction of accidents. There are a lot of things to know.

"From all the testimony that we (Ritter and his investigators) have given in court, we are recognized as expert witnesses before the court. As time goes on, with each sequential acknowledgment of that, it's a real feather in our hat, for that. It's gotten to the point where we train a lot of the local PDs (police departments) in it (homicide investigation) as well. In Volusia County, when there were investigations in some towns, like Deltona or DeBary, they would shadow us, as far as the investigations were going. They have roundtables with us, with some of their [investigation] problems, and have attended some of our schools in Tallahassee.

"Along the way, FHP came up with a team approach on investigation. I first got into the program," said Ritter, "in December 1986. And, when I was in St. Pete (rsburg), I had another homicide investigator who worked with me. A lot of times when I got called out, I was the only one that went. You were like the jack-of-all-trades when it came to that. It seemed like you had twenty arms pulling you twenty different directions—from between the medical examiner and the state attorney and people saying, 'Oh, I found this' and 'I found that,' they (FHP) realized there was a problem.

"Three sets of eyes are better than one. So, in the '90s, they initiated the team approach," he said. "They took just those who really wanted to remain, to stay actively involved in the homicide program, and they put them on a special squad. For instance, I have eight people who do nothing but homicide investigations. We handle all the cases in Seminole and Volusia Counties that fall under our jurisdiction. We have an on-call system where at nighttime, if there is a call, I have a minimum of two people who respond. That way, one may go off on one tangent and the other one goes off on another. Like I said, having another extra pair of eyes there may pick up on something the other person missed.

"Unfortunately, with crime scenes, such as in this particular case, all the evidence is very short-lived. If you don't document it before it is disturbed, it can really mess things up when it comes to your final determination. When you look at traffic homicide versus a shooting homicide, in most cases like that, people know who their assailant was, and a lot of times, the scene is very confined. On the other side of the coin, with our homicide investigation, you might have it stretched out over half-a-mile, and you don't know the perpetrator from Adam's house cat, and neither does the other person involved. It takes a lot of intuition and formative thinking, if you will, to go and find this [evidence], and reconstruct the scene.

"You can't take anything for granted, because it's like a wild snake," said Ritter. "It will rear up, and come up and strike you, if you miss the slightest thing—or even if you misinterpret the evidence. Corporal Wright really did an excellent job and we roundtabled that

[case]," discussing the investigation and conclusions. "When the state attorney's office hired a reconstructionist to review it, he agreed wholeheartedly with us, and he even suggested, for the most part, we were giving a lot of benefit of the doubt to the defendant. Which is what we always do anyway. That way, we are giving them all considerations available, and it's not like we are on a witch-hunt for them."

FHP homicide investigators have special training and Corporal Wright may have more than most. When he was quizzed by a defense attorney during a deposition on his qualifications to conduct a homicide investigation, he was able to list a number of specialized training schools he had attended, but his years of experience in investigation may have been the best teacher. In the most recent battle by defense attorney Timothy Berry, of Orlando, to convince the court to allow a new trial for Mary Hill, Wright told the attorney that "he would stand on his thirty-three years of experience" when his investigation report was questioned by Berry.

Because of the nature of traffic accidents, the scene is extremely fluid. It is much more difficult to secure a traffic homicide scene than it is to secure a scene in a locale such as a structure or even a park. Not only must roadways be speedily cleared for normal traffic to resume flow, it is difficult to keep the scene inviolate, because of the many people who may stop to aid victims or just to watch. Rescue teams themselves may unintentionally destroy evidence, trying to make a rescue, as well as the onlookers, who may not realize the scene is actually a crime scene. Traffic homicide investigators must work quickly to gather and secure evidence, to take photographs and interview witnesses. They may also have to analyze markings on roadways, which will soon disappear, as traffic or weather erodes them. . . . It helps to have an analytical mind and to be thorough. According to Sergeant Rick Ritter, head of the Deland homicide squad, Corporal Wright is both those things. "He's very thorough. He's good," said Ritter. Becoming a FHP homicide investigator is "pretty much a reward thing, a promotion," Ritter affirmed.

By August 7, 2000, Wright figured he had worked at least 135 homicide scenes as an investigator; that didn't even take into consideration scenes he worked other than as homicide investigator. He was dispatched to the Markham Woods Road crash at 4:36 P.M. and arrived on scene around 5:00 P.M.

By the time Wright arrived on scene, Mary Hill and Zak Rockwell had been transported by helicopter to ORMC. Dennis Hill was no longer there, although Wright would meet him a few days later in Hill's Wingfield North front yard, when he returned some items belonging to Mary and Amy that were retrieved from the scene.

Corporal Smith briefed him on the situation, Wright recalled. "Basically," he said, "it was a single vehicle crash into a fixed object resulting in two injuries and two fatalities." Smith also "related what I believe several witnesses had related to him about direction of travel and speed involved." Smith initially estimated the speed of the car at eighty miles per hour before the crash.

"When I arrived on the scene," said Wright, "I conferred with Corporal Smith. I asked for any information that he may have gathered. Corporal Templeton was in the process of photographing the scene. I reviewed the scene. I established physical evidence to support what I had been told in reference to the direction of travel and what had happened."

Physical evidence in a traffic crash can be varied. In this case, there was a lot of physical evidence to consider. "I located a set of furrow marks, a set of skid marks and a set of critical speed scuffs, and also a set of marks left by the car in the curve just north of the scene—which would have been acceleration marks, made possible by a weight shift in the vehicle."

Road marks become critical evidence at traffic crime scenes, as a trained investigator can determine what the vehicle was doing at the time the mark was established. The investigator cannot tell what the driver was thinking at the time, as Wright pointed out to a defense attorney questioning him during a deposition, but he can tell what the vehicle was doing when the mark was made. For instance, according to Wright, "a furrow mark is made by a wheel that is offering some resistance to dirt or gravel or any loose material, and as it implies, kind of creates a furrow through the soft material." In this particular crash, this is what happened on the shoulder of the west side of the road.

The experienced investigator, such as Wright, can even tell where a vehicle accelerates, by "reading" the markings. Acceleration marks are "characterized as a mark that is made by a weight shift in the vehicle," he said, "from its center of mass or center of gravity and the vehicle is still accelerating at that point." Those marks are "a very faint shadow, for lack of a better term."

His analysis of the markings he found that afternoon indicated that "the car was being driven at a high rate of speed and the driver of the vehicle was unable to maintain control over it. She overcorrected it. Then she overcorrected again."

In a deposition with some of Hill's former defense

attorneys (there had been a succession of them)—
Edward "Ted" Culhane and Gerald Boyle, at this point
in time—Culhane asked Wright for his opinion of
what happened. Based on his experience and careful
evaluation of the evidence, he could offer an opinion,
but wanted to ascertain they wanted it. "You want me
to tell what I think happened," he asked Culhane.

"Sure," Culhane replied.

Referring to his diagram of the crash scene, which
was part of the official investigative report, he explained, "I think that she accelerated around the
curve to the point that she was not capable or her ca-
pabilities of controlling the vehicle had been ex-
ceeded. Up to the Point D, she was still accelerating.
At that point, she probably said that 'I'm in trouble.
I've lost it.'

"I think that she left or took her foot off the gas and
kind of jerked it back to the right, which put her in
a clockwise rotation, and at one point, it was to such
a point that it was uncorrectable."

Culhane was curious as to how Wright had been
able to determine that the car was decelerating at
Point E on the diagram. "How were you able to determine that the car was decelerating?"

"Well," Wright said, "I took two readings starting at
Point E and going through about two-hundred feet
of it or through a two-hundred foot period and it
showed a deceleration rate. In other words, the radius
of the arch of—I believe that I used the left front tire
mark was decelerating.

"In other words, she was not accelerating. She was
decelerating at that point through the natural drive
factor of the vehicle." He doesn't believe there was any
acceleration from that point on.

The car was actually slowing down as it approached

the tree, as it was turning sideways. He was able to determine this by "the natural resistance of the tires sliding sideways, going from the critical-speed scuff mark, around a little bit further to a side scuff or deceleration or a skid mark, whichever you would like to refer to it."

When Culhane asked him if he found any indication of any skid marks that would be consistent with the brakes being applied, his reply was "No."

Also critical to the homicide investigation was the actual examination of the vehicle. Corporal Templeton took photographs of it at the scene, but Wright was only able to make a quick examination of it there. Next day, on Tuesday, August 8, 2000, he went to Altamonte Towing Company, in Altamonte Springs, where the vehicle was, and made a more thorough examination of it and photographed it in more detail.

"I photographed the vehicle, a little bit more in detail," he said. "I recorded the damage the best that I could. I checked the braking system, to see if there was any sign of a braking defect that I could say was prior to the collision."

One way to check this was by "seeing if there was any old brake fluid in the area of the cylinders of the wheel. If the pads to the calipers were in good shape or if the calipers had signs of gouging in them," it might reveal a mechanical failure. "I couldn't detect any mechanical failures with the vehicle.

"I also determined that the electrical system was damaged." He went back to the towing company a few days after that inspection of the vehicle, because he was curious about the crush damage to the car. The initial impact was to the left rear quarter panel at the left rear wheel. Wright reported in his official investigative report, there was approximately twenty-seven inches of inward crush at this point. The damaged area measured five feet three inches high and thirty-six inches wide, and extended from the rocker panel upward into the roof area.

"There is a way to determine speed from crush damage," he said, "several ways. I went back to see if there would be any way that I felt comfortable doing it." He decided to leave it to somebody else.

Wright's examination of the BMW revealed more destruction. Detached from the vehicle, in addition to the rear window, were the trunk lid, rear bumper cover and the front bumper cover. The front windshield was broken, the rear axle dislodged, with the right side extended nine inches outside the wheel well. The right rear door was sprung open, but would close. (This was the door that Jimmy Arthur opened, trying to reach the children inside the car.) The upper rear area of the driver's door was buckled outward, approximately fifteen inches. The sunroof was dislodged. Postcrash, the rear outside shoulder harnesses were cut in order for Zak and the girls' bodies to be removed.

One thing investigators do in an investigation of this nature is to pull up information from the National Highway Traffic Safety Administration (NHTSA) Web site, to see if there are consumer complaints about a particular vehicle. "I didn't see any recalls," he said.

Often evidence would involve something other than the vehicle and road markings. In this case, a beer bottle was found at the scene, but later dismissed as not being relevant to the crash. Still, it was photographed and noted in his report. At first investigation, it was not known by the FHP squad investigating the crash scene, whether it was relevant or not.

What was considered relevant was the presence of pill bottles. "One bottle was in her (Mary Hill's) purse," Wright recalled. He noted in his official report that he found the purse next to the tree that the car crashed into. One pill bottle was found on the front car seat. He took pictures of those, too. Wright determined that both prescriptions contained less than they should have, if taken as directed. For this reason, when he saw her at ORMC, he requested that Mary Hill submit to a blood test. The blood was drawn and submitted to Florida Department of Law Enforcement (FDLE) in Orlando, and later showed to have only a breakdown of nordiazepam, a chemical waste or by-product of the antianxiety drug Valium. The two prescription bottles found at the crash scene were for Serzone, an antidepressant and antianxiety drug, and for Klonopin, used to treat mood disorders. Attorney Ted Culhane told the media that his client, Mary Hill, was not under the influence of any substance on the day of the crash, supported by the presence of the drug breakdown from prior consumption, and not on the day of the crash.

A mid-September 2000 interview with Zak Rockwell revealed little about the crash. All he could recall for Corporal Wright was the car rotating as it traveled toward the tree and the trees going by very fast.

After an extensive investigation, Corporal Wright came to the following conclusions in his report—that Mary Hill was the primary contributor to the crash. In crashing her vehicle, he concluded that she violated two counts of Florida Law: State Statute 782.071, vehicular homicide. In his report, he described vehicular homicide as "the killing of a human being, caused by the operation of a motor vehicle by another in a reckless manner likely to cause the death of, or great bodily harm to, another." Wright maintained that Hill was operating her vehicle in such a reckless manner that it ended in the traffic crash that caused the deaths of two children, Amy Hill and Carrie Brown, and caused "serious bodily injury" to a third child, Zak Brown.

In the report, he also cited Hill for violation of Florida State Statute 316.614 (4)(b). Generically termed the Seat Belt Law, it specifies that a driver may not operate a motor vehicle without wearing a seat belt. He would write, "It is unlawful for any person to operate a motor vehicle in this state unless the person is restrained by a safety belt."

He concluded his report by indicating that the investigation was complete and that he, as the homicide investigator, had obtained a warrant or capias for the arrest of the defendant.

Corporal Wright turned in his completed investigative report with his findings and recommendations on October 5, 2000, although Mary Hill would not be arrested until Tuesday, April 3, 2001. Jim Carter, assistant state attorney (ASA), who was the Seminole County supervisor for felony intake at the time (now in private practice in Lake County), brought in his own accident reconstruction specialist, Hans Fuehrer, to check the conclusions of the FHP investigative report. Fuehrer first saw the scene seven months after the crash, and tire marks from the crash were still visible. Carter was cautious. He knew in order for the state attorney's office to prosecute the case successfully, it would need to prove that Mary Hill's driving was so reckless, it was bound to kill or seriously injure someone. According to Carter, he had an "ethical obligation not to file something I can't prove." The state attorney's office did issue a warrant for

Mary Hill's arrest almost nine months after the fatal crash. She would spend two hours in jail, posting bond, and then went back home to Wingfield North, the gates closing behind her, shutting her in to live in her own reality, or her own hell, a virtual recluse.

Mary Hill was charged with vehicular homicide and manslaughter for the deaths of Carrie Brown and her own daughter Amy Hill. After Mary Hill and Zak Rockwell had been airlifted to ORMC for treatment, the bodies of the two girls remained in the vehicle. When they were removed from the car, they were transported to the medical examiner's office in Volusia County for autopsy. Dr. Thomas R. Parsons, Volusia County medical examiner (ME), listed Amy's cause of death as multiple blunt-force injuries. The more severe injuries were listed as a hinge fracture that extended from the left temporal bone and terminated in the right temporal bone. Fractures of the left clavicle, fractures of many ribs and a pulmonary contusion were listed, along with lacerations to the liver, bladder and spleen. Pelvic ring fractures and numerous superficial abrasions were evident.

Dr. Thomas R. Beaver conducted Carrie's autopsy. Cause of death was listed as multiple fractures and internal injuries due to blunt force. He reported fractures to the left ribs, left clavicle, pelvis and a basilar skull fracture. Also listed were injuries to the left lung, spleen and numerous abrasions.

A viewing for Amy Hill was held Thursday, August 10, 2000, at the Church of the Nativity, Longwood. A mass was held on Friday, August 11, 2000, with burial in Cobden, Illinois.

A viewing and wake service for Carrie Brown was held on Friday, August 11, 2000. A mass was held the next day at the Church of Annunciation in Longwood.

Burial was in Des Plaines, Illinois, on Monday, August 14, 2000.

A charge of aggravated negligence for Zak Rockwell's injuries would be added later in the state's case against Mary Hill, in a ploy to force the testimony of husband Dennis Hill and of Sanford psychiatrist Eduard Gfeller, who saw her the day of the crash.

CHAPTER 8

No one is truly free, they are a slave to wealth,
fortune, the law, or other people restraining
them from acting according to their will.
                                        —Euripides

If anyone thought that the FHP investigative report
on the crash would put an end to all the questions of
"why?" and "how?" a new wrinkle would develop in the
case. Dennis and Mary Hill's defense team came up
with an alternative reason of their own for the crash
cause.

Dennis Hill hired high-profile defense attorneys
to defend his wife and to promote the out-of-control
cruise control defense. In January 2002, local defense
attorney Ted Culhane, at one time a prosecuting attorney himself, was joined by nationally known defense
attorney Gerald Boyle, famous for defending serial
killer and cannibal, Jeffrey Dahmer, at a deposition.
They questioned FHP Corporal Phillip C. Wright extensively about the car crash and what may have
caused it. By this time, ASA Jim Carter had left the
office and had been replaced by Pat Whitaker as

felony intake supervisor in Seminole County. Pat Whitaker assumed the role as lead prosecutor in the Mary Hill case, now known as case number 01-1217-CFA, *The State of Florida, plaintiff,* v. *Mary Louise Hill, defendant.* It was a number that would receive a lot of use, as the initial trial was followed by many hearings, an appeal for a new trial, and still pending, the appeal to the Fifth District Court in Daytona Beach to overturn the verdict of the first trial and to set a new trial.

Culhane and Boyle were setting the scene for a spectacular defense: Mary Hill wasn't driving the car, the car was driving itself. She and her passengers were all victims of the car itself, something like *Christine,* the Stephen King horror novel and movie. They were all the victims of a car manufactured by BMW: Mary Hill was a victim; Amy Hill was a victim; Carrie Brown was a victim; Zak Rockwell was a victim. The real culprit was going to be BMW.

They had to come up with a way to prove their theory. One way would be to attempt to abrogate Wright's findings. They would also bring forward other BMW drivers who were willing to testify in court that their BMWs took over control of their driving as well. A popular ride for children at nearby Disney World, until a few years ago, was Mr. Toad's Wild Ride. Hill's attorneys were setting up a scenario where riding in certain BMWs was no less a wild ride.

Culhane quizzed Wright about whether or not he had looked into consumer complaints concerning cruise control problems with BMWs. "Do you know whether there was a recall of 1995 or 1997 cruise controls in BMWs?" he asked.

"I don't know of any" was Wright's reply.

Culhane went right to the heart of what the defense was proposing: "For my next series of questions, I will have to include this, but I will, for the purposes of asking you this question, let you know that we have two witnesses who have had problems with cruise controls in BMWs. One of whom had a cruise control which suddenly engaged and started to 'red line' into seventy-five-thousand RPMs, and when he stepped on the brake, it didn't work. And, as in this one, the person who . . . when they stepped on the brake, the cruise control accelerated.

"Now, based on either one of those scenarios, where the cruise control suddenly engaged and made the car accelerate, essentially, as fast as it could go, or a situation where the cruise control was engaged, and when they stepped on the brake, the cruise control, rather than disengaging, suddenly accelerated—would that be consistent with what you saw in the course of the examination of the scene here?"

Wright wasn't cooperating with the theory. "The only thing that I can elaborate on the scene of the crash is what I've recorded and my observations and experience indicates to me that the first mark was an acceleration mark. Further testimony by witnesses would indicate this was a pattern of the driver in the way that she was driving this vehicle, prior to this scene of the crash."

Culhane accepted that answer without discussion, but Wright elaborated. "This is almost," he said, "both of these are almost textbook of an acceleration mark due to a vehicle accelerating and starting to rotate and the overreaction. I guess the question in my mind would be, if the cruise control had engaged, why was she decelerating at this point, because the striations and the marks on the pavement would be of a rotating tire?" He described marks left on the pavement that indicated that the vehicle was slowing.

Wright said the speed at Point E on the diagram was calculated to be seventy-two miles per hour. When Culhane, referring to the same diagram, asked him about the speed at Point G, Wright told him it would have been about the same, but somewhat less, not much. "You are not going to really have that much deceleration through a lot of that because you don't have that much coefficient, braking coefficient or deceleration factor involved in this because you are not applying the brake," Wright explained. "That's just the weight shift in the vehicle turning causing the friction between the tire and the road and the cause of the scorching of the pavement."

Culhane pressed on: "So, do you have an estimate, though, of what the speed was at the time that the car hit the tree?"

"Do you want an estimate?" asked Wright. His estimate when Culhane said "Yes" was "probably around forty-five."

"Well," said Culhane, "in one of our situations that we have with the report of a problem with the cruise control, on three different occasions, as the person stepped on the brake, the cruise control accelerated." When Wright inquired whether or not that individual was Mary Hill, Culhane admitted, it was someone else who had the problem.

"I was going to say," said Wright, "if she had it (the problem), why didn't she take it and have it corrected, or evidently, it was doing that back on Lake Mary Boulevard, according to one of the witnesses."

"I don't know whether it occurred before," said Culhane.

"Myself, I would have jumped out of the car and left it there," Wright said.

Culhane related two different accounts of BMWs

having cruise controls engaging and accelerating on their own. Hitting the brake seemed to his witnesses to be the cause of the acceleration. He asked Wright, "If Mrs. Hill had a sudden acceleration and was able to hit the brake, whether it left a skid mark or not, and suddenly disengaged the cruise control, would that be consistent with this pattern?"

"From what I can gather from the witnesses," Wright reminded him, "that moments before the crash occurred, she braked the vehicle at a fast rate.

"I mean, it has to be considered," he continued, "because it's a driving pattern. What I am trying to do is paint the picture in my own mind, that if she suddenly backed the vehicle, after stopping it in the intersection, and then those two witnesses that were in the vehicle behind her, plus a third that was on a bicycle, saw an instantaneous acceleration, not only an instantaneous acceleration, but an anticipation of the light turning, as a person who is obviously in a great hurry to creep into the intersection, waiting for the light to turn green—and then, all of a sudden, there's rapid acceleration and then within several seconds later, you have a wreck. . . . I guess it would depend on if they were accelerating from a stop. If they had engaged the cruise control while they were, let's say, highway speed, I'm not sure."

Culhane maintained Hill's continued tapping of the brake at the intersection triggered the cruise control to accelerate. Wright could not recall that any witnesses saw the brake lights flash after she left the intersection.

"From the time that she accelerated from the intersection of Lake Mary and Markham Woods to the time that she went around the curb," said Wright, "there probably would be some point that they lost sight of her, but they did see her hit the tree. It depends on what area that they lost sight and if they did see any brake lights come on."

Culhane pushed again, while Boyle remained quiet through the questioning. "Okay. Well, if she was stopped at the stoplight and creeping into the intersection when the light—standing on her brakes, or stepping on her brakes, and then when the light turned green, it triggered an acceleration from the cruise control, engaging like these other people have had; would the information that you testified to today be consistent with that happening also as a plausible alternative theory?"

"I would hate to venture a guess on how much of an acceleration rate that you would have," Wright responded. "If it was an absolutely maximum acceleration, this car has quite an acceleration rate. I know that it's more so than our patrol cars have. It's from zero to sixty in 7.2 seconds at 12.2 feet per second with a per second of g force of .38. That's probably comparable to our old Mustangs. It exceeds our Crown Vics."

Wright quizzed Culhane himself: "Does the NHTSA fact sheet say if it was total acceleration or a moderate or light? Because it is an interesting area." Culhane read the fact sheet data to Wright. "I guess it would depend on," Wright said, "well, there would be so many factors. I would hate to tell you how many times people have told me that they have put their foot on the brake and hit the gas pedal, instead, and driven into stores."

Culhane agreed that could have happened, but asked, "But, could what I just said have occurred, too?"

Wright agreed that there was a possibility that it could have happened, but relying on the facts of his investigation, "in this particular scenario, I don't think that it happened that way (Culhane's way)."

Although Culhane continued to attempt to sway Wright into admitting he was correct in his theory that the cruise control accelerated out of control, Wright came back to the findings of his investigation. "But we still have the fact that, from here to there to there (referring to the diagram), you have deceleration . . . without the brakes being applied."

Culhane said, "Right, but if she had successfully tapped the brake and disengaged it and not stood on the brakes, it would be consistent with that, too."

"What would you have done," Wright asked, "if you were going out of control? Would you let up off the brakes?"

Culhane told him, "I hate to be this way, but what I am going to be is chauvinistic. It's my experience that women panic in situations like this. A man would know to turn the ignition off."

"Not all of them," Wright responded. "Different people react to different situations in different ways. I don't hold anybody to the same standard that I hold myself, because I consider myself, after thirty-one years, I am not a race car driver, but I do consider myself more experienced than the majority of the people out here on the highway. So, I wouldn't expect them to react to a situation the same way that I would."

Culhane related an incident one of the BMW drivers had related to him. "I can tell you that the owner of the second car indicated to me that it scared him to death, and he was expecting it. The one, when he stepped on the pedal, and it came up and suddenly accelerated, he essentially didn't know what to do at first, the first time it happened to him—and his wife had already told him that it happened.

"Would you think that would be a plausible situation from a person that has never had it happen before?"

"If it would have been me," Wright told him, "I would have taken the thing in right away when my wife told me that the cruise control, or it (the car), was accelerating for whatever reason."

"Unless it killed you the first time," Culhane shot back.

"Yeah," Wright said. "The only thing that I can say, sir, is the physical evidence at the scene indicates that there was acceleration here. There was a deceleration there and that the surface marks here were indicative of no braking from a free-rolling tire."

Culhane, to the objection of Whitaker, kept pressing Wright to go along with his theory. After a number of objections, Culhane said, "My rephrased question is, if the cruise control stuck when she stepped on the brakes at that light, and that's the reason that she crashed into the tree, then she wouldn't be guilty of this offense, would she?"

Whitaker objected again, saying that was asking Wright to give a legal opinion.

Culhane tried again: "Would there be probable cause if you knew that the—if you found out that the cruise control stuck, and that's the reason that she accelerated, would there be probable cause to arrest her, if you had known that at the time, or shortly after the accident?"

"Yes, sir" was Wright's immediate reply.

"You would have still arrested her?"

"Yes, sir."

"Why is that?" Culhane asked.

"Anybody that would drive a vehicle with that much power with a cruise control sticking, with three young children in the back—"

"What if it was the first time?"

Culhane pressed and pressed his point, not swaying Wright to abandon the facts of his investigation report. Wright pointed out to Culhane: "The question I would ask myself in the reconstruction is, if it did stick, why didn't it continue to stick?

"In my opinion," Wright told Culhane as the wrangling continued, "I don't think that the cruise control had anything to do with it."

Culhane didn't give up. "Okay, but you don't know that, do you?"

"The only thing that I am certain about," Wright said, "is what I have elaborated on in the report."

Wright's report focused on what happened from the time Mary Hill's BMW left the intersection of Lake Mary Boulevard—after the traffic light switched to green—and hit a large, live oak tree growing between the sidewalk and Markham Woods Road . . . a distance of $\frac{1}{10}$ mile.

Eighteenth Judicial Circuit judge O. H. Eaton Jr., who presided over the vehicular homicide/manslaughter trial in 2004, would reiterate that fact in a defense appeal for a new trial. The defense team based that appeal on new witnesses coming forward, who, they maintained, would have changed the outcome of the original trial. All that mattered, Judge Eaton said, was what occurred in that $\frac{1}{10}$ mile from the intersection to the tree.

One-tenth of a mile, $\frac{1}{10}$ of a mile, $\frac{1}{10}$ th mile, regardless of how you write it or how you say it, it's a short distance that was traveled with a far-reaching effect . . . not only in the lives taken away, the lives changed, but in how Mary Hill got to the state she was in, the day she drove her car on a deadly trip. Her journey there was a long one.

CHAPTER 9

When desire dies, fear is born.
                    —Baltasar Gracian

Mary Hill was not always the woman known to many newspaper readers, television newscast watchers and viewers of the news feature show *48 Hours Investigates*. The woman whom those people came to know seemed tired, at times defeated, only occasionally defiant, always remote. She barely spoke above a whisper. During her testimony, she had to be prompted to speak up so she could be heard. Her very appearance was a ghost of the person she once was. It was apparent her clothes were expensive, but they were a little dowdy. Mary Hill looked a little matronly, in her tailored suits, clinging to an outmoded "Alice in Wonderland" hairstyle, reminiscent of a longer version of the style of Jean Harris, the woman who was accused and convicted in the slaying of her former lover, Scarsdale Diet doctor Herman Tarnower. She, too, had presented a cool, matronly image in court. Unlike Jean Harris, postcrash Mary Hill was a far cry from Mary Hill precrash.

The precrash Mary Hill would sweep through the phone room of Barbara Nolan Market Research in her latest high-fashion, designer outfit—including designer shoes and accessories. She favored flashy diamond jewelry—sometimes wearing a diamond-encrusted necklace given to her by husband Dennis Hill, according to a former household employee. The diamond necklace spelled out the words "Rich Bitch," and she was fond of telling employees, "I am both."

Former Barbara Nolan employee Willis Towne recalled she liked to make the crew aware of when she was coming and going. "It was like a display. It was kind of sickening. She would walk out through the back, instead of going out the front. You know, parading through the building, where the five-dollar-an-hour employees work. She liked to flaunt her money, they both did. I guess when you have that much, you just get that way.

"I would assume they were megawealthy. I heard rumors about planes, boats, an island, so I guess the extravagance goes with that."

Towne said, "She wasn't at all like the figure you see on TV and at the trial now. She was beautiful. She was very thin and some of us worried for her health, because she would be so thin. She was almost anorexic. She kept herself well—her hair was always done, she would wear designer clothes, designer shoes, the whole thing." Towne was amazed at her taste in jewelry, compared to the rest of her fashion ensemble. "She would wear big, gaudy diamond jewelry with them."

Pat Key remembered the "Rich Bitch" necklace. "I'm not sure it had real diamonds on it." But former nanny Deane David confirmed it was covered with real diamonds and that Dennis Hill had the piece created for Mary. The necklace was like designs that could be purchased in the late '80s and early '90s at many mall boutiques—they were flashy, a little trashy, a fun piece of costume jewelry. But if Deane David is correct, Mary Hill's little bauble was worth more than a few bucks, and was definitely not purchased at a mall's costume jewelry shop. Dennis Hill purchased some of David's own jewelry to give to his wife after David began working for them.

Mary Hill had very expensive jewelry. After the crash, when she was convalescing at home, she employed a well-known home-nursing company to supply caregivers to assist her. One of the nursing aides they sent to her home, stole more than $100,000 worth of jewelry, mostly made of gold and diamonds, from a jewelry box on her dresser, plus her wedding ring from the bath area.

Mary Hill didn't report the theft, which occurred in November 2000, until July 2001. She told deputies she had not reported it on the advice of her attorneys, because of a traumatic situation the family had suffered. The SCSO deputies' report stated that she told them that she suspected one of the aides of stealing her jewelry while her mental/physical condition was impaired. The suspected woman was subsequently arrested for the theft, on a charge of grand larceny, first degree over $100,000. The most expensive items were a diamond-and-gold-necklace valued at $48,774, a diamond bracelet valued at $9,000 and a diamond ring valued at $8,500. Less expensive items ranged from a $1,800 sapphire-and-diamond ring to her $2,650 diamond wedding ring—not exactly costume trinkets purchased at a mall kiosk.

Mary Hill loved to shop, especially for designer clothes, which she often purchased at bargain prices. One favorite Winter Park boutique was often the beneficiary of her late-afternoon shopping sprees. Reportedly, she would dash in right at closing time, just as the owner and employees were preparing to leave for the day. She would tear through the store, buying anything, and everything, that caught her fancy. Clothes and purses—there seemed to be no particular structure to the trip or purchases. It was nothing for her to drop $5,000 in a shopping spree. It was always a good payday for the boutique owner, who didn't mind the inconvenience of the timing of her client, or a little complaining from employees. It was well worth the effort spent to cater to the wealthy woman.

Former employee Marge Burns recalled Mary Hill bringing in all kinds of presents at Christmastime that she had purchased for Amy and Kaitlynn. "She would be showing them off to the employees. 'Look what I bought Amy,' or 'Look what I bought for Kaitlynn,' and here we were, making six dollars or less an hour."

Key recalled, "At Christmastime, she would bring all the gifts into the office and keep them there so the kids couldn't find them; yet she made a great point of showing them to us—what she had bought them, gifts that cost hundreds of dollars, and going, 'Oh, look, I went to New York and got Amy this,' and 'Amy that,' and we're all going, 'It must be nice.'" When asked if she actually did go to New York on shopping trips, no one knew. All they knew was, she wasn't around the office a lot, and no one knew where she went.

Burns recalled that in the face of this largesse, nothing was done for the employees at Christmas—no bonuses, no gifts, not even a Christmas card. "When someone pointed out to her this wasn't a good thing, she hurriedly threw together a Christmas party at their mansion for all of us lowly employees. Not that we didn't want to see the place, we had heard enough about it."

"Right," said Key, "like the tennis court and putting green. They didn't even know how to play tennis. It was all a thing to impress everyone. It was only after the accident, you know, that her physical appearance changed. Until then, she was like 'Ms. Society,' it was stuff like this—they bought a house in Heathrow, but it wasn't big enough, so they bought a bigger house." His impression was that Heathrow wasn't exclusive enough for them anymore. "It wasn't exclusive like it used to be, so they moved. One house had a media room with a drop-down screen and Mary loved it. But it wasn't good enough. So, they moved to the big house in Wingfield North. They bought a house with a tennis court—the thing is neither one of them played tennis. They bought a house with a tennis court, just for the status of it.

"Dennis has a little tiny duplex next to the old office in Altamonte. He bought it originally to tear down for more parking, but decided instead it would be better to rent out." Key was amazed at how much he was able to rent it for. He was getting pretty good money for it. "When Mary and Dennis had the big split, last I heard, Dennis was living in that house." Key speculated it no longer mattered whether or not Dennis and Mary Hill knew how to play tennis . . . the court Mary would be facing had nothing to do with playing games or having fun.

Burns recalled the Christmas party they all went to in Wingfield North. "Everything was beautifully decorated. The tree was huge. There was lots of food. One of the women from Barbara Nolan did a lot of Mary's catering for her, she was like a close friend, and there was a huge assortment of food. One thing that sticks out in my mind, though, was Amy and Kaitlynn playing the pianos (the mansion housed two large grand pianos). You could tell they really didn't want to do it, but they played anyway.

"Here's the difference in two women," said Burns. "I worked off and on for the company back when Barbara Nolan actually owned it. And I sometimes worked there when the Hills owned it. I didn't have any reason to believe she (Nolan) even knew who I was.

"After the Hills bought the company, they kept the name, because the name had integrity in the marketing business, something that was slipping with U.S. Research Company because of a few borderline-type practices they were doing. One was not paying [to] people surveyed the money that was promised them for turning in a completed marketing survey or product trial. The Hills would get the money from their client, but it was really hard for people (the public) who did the survey to get the money from the marketing company. They were beginning to do some of the same things with surveys conducted by the Barbara Nolan branch of the business. When people would turn in their results, expecting to get whatever they had been promised, they would be told they had to make the request to U.S. Research. They would be given a real runaround; they would delay, delay, until a lot of them just gave up. It might not have amounted to much on an individual basis, but it was just more money in the Hills' pockets.

"Anyway, remember how Mary Hill had to be 'reminded' to do something for the employees for Christmas? Here's what Barbara Nolan was like. I was at the food court at one of the malls one day and she walked right up to me. This was after she had retired from the business. 'You're Marge, aren't you?'

she asked. I didn't even know she knew who I was, let alone would ever remember my name.

"'Would you like an ice cream cone?' she asked me. She actually paid for it. Now, that's a classy woman for you. What a difference."

Pat Key was quick to point out that "Mary Hill was the queen bee at Barbara Nolan. Her name was never spoken without her last name. It was one word, Mary-Hill. If something had to be done by someone, the key words, or word, was 'MaryHill said to . . .' or 'Mary-Hill told me to tell you to . . .'

"She had a few close people she worked with, and those were the people she socialized with. If she ever socialized with anyone else, it never got out that she did.

"It was like they were the nouveau riche, they came from nothing and they flaunted it (their wealth) in front of people," Key said. "Some people are impressed by it, some people are distressed by it, and some just go, 'I already have that.' Why else buy a house with a tennis court, when you don't play tennis? It just doesn't make sense.

"Mary was a total trip," Key said on the *48 Hours* episode. "When you see that thing there with her crying, and I love it when you see her there crossing herself. They weren't religious. Maybe she grew up Catholic, but that's part of the facade."

Deane David also was puzzled by the show of religion. "I am very religious," said Deane. "If I brought up the subject of God to Mary, she was like, 'Where was God when my father was killed when I was twelve? Don't talk to me about God.'"

Possibly, the trauma the family went through after Amy's death caused a renewal of faith in them.

Administrative personnel at their church in Longwood remembered them as "a lovely family."

Jennifer Wilson, Mary's daughter, remembered a
different woman—a woman none of the marketing
employees or household employees ever knew. Many
of her memories of her mother are tangled up in
memories of Dennis Hill.

Her biological father, divorced by Mary Hill when
Jennifer was a toddler, never had much impact in her
day-to-day life. "He [Dennis Hill] has been my dad my
whole life," Jennifer said of Dennis Hill, trying to explain their relationship. "Yet, he was never a dad to
me. He would never accept me as a daughter. Financially he took care of me. Whenever I needed anything, he was always there, but as for emotional
support or being a parent of any kind, no. He was only
financially there if my mother pressured him to be so."
Apparently Mary Hill didn't pressure him to pay for
Jennifer's wedding, depending on her fiance's parents
to pick up the tab.

Jennifer Wilson had known Dennis Hill a long
time. He had been part of her life for a long time.
"They got married when I was eight and we still lived
in Mt. Prospect, Illinois. We lived there for a little
while, and when I was thirteen years old, my mom got
pregnant with Amy, and my dad's business turned in
a very beneficial direction and started to really sky-
rocket for him—he is an extreme workaholic.

"He [Dennis Hill] is this driven, self-made millionaire.
Those are things I have always respected of him," she
said. "He made himself from the bottom up. But it just
became everything. He became motivated by the money
and the power and then we moved to Barrington, which
is like the Heathrow/Alaqua of our area (in central
Florida)—very much an exclusive, upscale area."

Although financially, the life of the Hills was on an upswing, the family unit was under pressure, extreme pressure, personally. Jennifer thinks that Dennis began to pay less attention to Mary at that point; his attention diverted elsewhere. She doesn't understand why. "When my mother was young, she was so beautiful."

Photographs of Mary Hill prior to the August 2000 crash show a vibrant, beautiful woman, who exudes "movie star" glamour. In fact, in some pictures, she looks very much like a blond movie queen, her style popular in the 1940s and 1950s.

Jennifer described Dennis's obsession with Mary: "'The most beautiful woman,' he (Dennis) would tell you. She was the most beautiful woman he had ever seen, or hoped to see and be with. But after he married her, Mary Hill's daughter feels her mother apparently wasn't enough for him.

"My mom was what I guess you would call arm candy for him, and his greatest conquest. He really, truly did love her in the beginning." All did not remain well between Mary and Dennis Hill. Eventually, a judge granted a restraining order against Dennis Hill based on Mary Hill's description of violent abuse he directed towards her.

But in the Hills' early years together, Mary apparently thought flight was better than involving the courts. "My mom was seeing this," Jennifer said, "and didn't want to deal with it. I think that was really the turn for her to move to Florida after Kaitlynn was born. Absolutely, the reason she was taking the drugs and drinking was because of what he was doing. My mom never drank, ever. But when she started, he would say, 'If one won't help, Mary, take two,' until she would go away. It started like that. He started her into other areas, places she didn't want to go." Jennifer was reluctant to talk about the sexual life of her parents, although it was apparent she was struggling to deal with that knowledge.

"Anyway, she moved to Florida and started working at Barbara Nolan, which is an extension of his company, and she started at the bottom to learn the business. She wanted to work again and wanted to feel useful, have a purpose again, and have her own money. She started at the bottom literally, working at focus groups, like I started working, at the bottom. Dennis was running the business at this time, and Barbara Nolan was still there, until she decided to retire, although she had sold it" to the Hills. Mary kept learning the business. She took over Barbara Nolan Market Research when Barbara Nolan finally left. "It was shortly after that, that my mom started running it. After she moved to Florida, Dennis had a child with a woman in Illinois. He refused and still refuses, to this day, to relinquish or terminate that relationship, no matter what my mom did.

"My mother, very much, so tried to get him to give this other woman up. And he would not do so. There were talks of divorce." But Jennifer felt her mother was reluctant to pursue it. The fear of divorce was a major fear for her, because he would withdraw all support.

"She had been there before and didn't want to go back there again. I don't know the whole reason of her holding on there [to the Hill marriage]." Jennifer recalls receiving a phone call from her mom, after she learned of the birth of the child. It was a call theat ended her college career. "This was way prior to the accident. He would only travel down to Florida every other or every two weekends.

"When Dennis moved back to Florida after Amy died, that's when he permanently moved here. Most of the time, he was in Illinois with [his mistress], but he didn't live there with her full-time, because she is married herself.

"Believe it or not, she is a very, very nice woman. I have known her my whole life and cannot say a bad thing about her, regardless of the affair or anything. I still cannot say a bad thing about her. She is very even-tempered and she is a good businessperson— just a very nice person. I don't get it. Between her and my mother, I just don't understand [the attraction to Dennis Hill].

"It was horrible for my mother when the child was born," she says. "His other kids were so mad at him," too. She recalls stepsisters Julie and Heather being very upset over the birth and that stepbrother Dennis seemed to ignore Dennis Sr. for awhile after that.

"I was finished with him [Dennis] at this point. He was already a disgusting person to me. I had just started to wash my hands of him. But, he's still my dad, and I still wanted him in my life, because he's my dad. Those guys [three other children from the first marriage] have always hated my mother. She was the other woman. She was blamed for the breakup of the marriage. They were having an affair, but it wasn't the [his] only one. They just hated her. They were just evil to each other."

To the bitter conclusion of the case, that animosity seemed to continue. Two of Dennis's older children from his first marriage, Julie and Heather, made an appearance on the *48 Hours* episode about the case, "Driven to Extremes," where they stated they had ridden with Mary Hill, in fear of their lives after she became angry at their dad.

Mary's relationship with the three older Hill children was very volatile. One time when Dennis Jr. was living at the first Wingfield North residence of the Hills on Vista Oak, they got into what amounted to a slapping match, and the sheriff's office was called. A domestic violence report was filled out.

"The girls [Julie and Heather] never lived with them, but came [to visit] from time to time. At first, they spent more weekends, until their early teens, like freshman or sophomore [school years] was the last time I really remember them coming over on the weekends. And that was that. They stopped doing that altogether.

"Dennis wasn't really a dad to them, either. He would rather go read a book than spend time with them." Although he was frequently remote to his family, Jennifer said, "Dennis loves to be the focus, the center of attention, that's where the piano playing comes in. He's very good at the piano."

Deane David, a former nanny, has been very vocal, and public, about her work relationship with the Hills, revealing an insider's view of what went on in Dennis and Mary Hill's household. "I think Deane David is a liar. I don't know, I've met Deane maybe three or four times in my entire life and the last time I spoke with her—and I maybe have only spoken to her one more time than that—she called the house and I had to request that she not call here ever again," Jennifer said. "She was going on and on to Kaitlynn about inappropriate things, and a fabricated story about her and I going to a party together. I've never been anywhere with Deane in my life. Kaitlynn was staring at me while she was going on with this elaborate lie. My question is 'Why? For what reason?' There was no gain for a lie. Why would you go on about this elaborate story that never happened? What personal gain could she get out of it?

"For instance, I had been to one of the parties my parents had hosted, and Deane was introducing herself as my mother. It was bizarre. She was a bizarre lady. At first she and my mom got along; then it turned ugly.

"The drug use had started to become visual and Mom was becoming unhappier. My dad wouldn't let her work anymore and he wouldn't come down here anymore. The thing with [his mistress] wouldn't go away.

"For a time, she [Mary] tried something radical, for which I told myself, 'She is absolutely going to crack. This isn't normal.' But she would tell us, 'He has his life there, and we have our life here, and as long as I have what I have . . .'

"I was like, 'What?' No one could understand." In the end, "it just didn't work for her, and finally she got disgusted with the whole thing. I guess the drugs weren't making her happy anymore and she couldn't get herself happy anymore, and when you're not happy, there's no amount of anything that is going work," Jennifer said.

"Then there was the going to psychiatrists. If one said something that somebody—I don't know if it was Dennis or Mom—but if they didn't like it, they would go again to another one. And then it just seemed an endless [quest]. There was no honesty—no calling a spade a spade. You know, not saying one was worse than the other, but you both really need to get away from each other. Your self-destructive personalities are out of control; you with your [drug/alcohol] addictions, you with your sexual addictions, and you're gonna hurt somebody. And they did.

"When this all came around, Dennis thought he was going to sue BMW. When the truth comes down to it, I don't know if the car failed. I do know she didn't mean to kill anybody. That's the only thing I do know. Let it be a freak accident—a stupid, out-of-control accident. Or, really let it be the car's fault. These are some of [the] things I have no idea [of] the answer for, but you don't decide at that point, I don't care if the car was at fault or not—don't make profit out of your child's death, and that's all Dennis could talk about . . . suing BMW. He really pushed and pushed and pushed, and I think that's the point that my mom didn't care.

"She had now slipped into a 'just want to die mode' and that's when the drinking starts. After Amy died, she would start drinking. She blamed herself, and, of course, my dad hated her and blamed her. He was along shortly after it happened and said terrible things to her.

"He brought Heather, Dennis and Julie down [after the crash]. They attacked my mother frequently about how she killed her (Amy). They would say, 'She's a fucking murderer'; 'You're going to hell.' And these are kids who didn't know Amy very much at all. I mean, they were her sisters and brother, and deserved the right to be there, but never did he step up once and say, 'We're not going to make this issue worse. This is Amy's day. Those may be your true feelings, but you keep your mouth shut. Don't make this issue worse. Or you can't be here.' You know, do the respectable thing. He didn't need to defend her, but he didn't have to let them do that. He didn't have to buy their tickets to let them be on *48 Hours,* to let them talk trash.

"Don't make the situation worse. Be there to mourn the death of your sister, the death of your daughter; don't be there to get in somebody's face. That's not what it was supposed to be about. And that was what it was about. And before the *48 Hours* thing, if you are going to do something, do something to remember those kids. Cherish those children, you know.

"It's like I told the *Orlando Sentinel* (the major area daily newspaper), who wouldn't leave me alone, 'If you are going to do something to tell other families that are like mine, like Carrie Brown's, how do we get through this? How do I deal with this? How can you prevent your family to getting to this point? If you have a family like mine, if you can write one piece on something that would do something good, I will talk to you. But if all you want to do is take the littlest, dirtiest thing I say and print it, you never want to say it's a terrible tragedy and that's all you care about. You know, you can say this is a terrible tragedy and don't let it happen to you; there are outreach programs, there are outreach places.' That's what I asked (of them).

"I saw my dad in those interviews (*48 Hours*), and I've never seen such a fake act in my life. It was so . . . he's not playing [the piano] every night to Amy's picture. I know for a fact he's not. I can show you dozens and dozens of e-mails we have received saying he's at this place and that place, and we are going to go here. . . . You know it's crap. Yes, he totally misses his daughter, don't take that out of context, that he doesn't truly miss her, and doesn't mourn her death, but that on TV was fake. We all just sat there looking at each other and shaking our heads, like going, 'Huh? Huh?'"

CHAPTER 10

For many men, the acquisition of wealth does not
end their troubles, it only changes them.

—Seneca

Dennis Hill, husband of Mary Hill, is one of the
most enigmatic individuals encountered in the Mary
Hill case. Almost no one has had anything good to say
about him—yet the people who could say some wonderful things (people who were beneficiaries of his
largesse, such as Charles Moore, Amy's music teacher,
and Rolann Owens, Amy and Kaitlynn's dance
teacher) have refused to talk about any of the Hills.
Their silence has left an unanswered mystery regarding the man.

Former Barbara Nolan employee Marge Burns said
Dennis "is an all right kind of guy," although having not
one good thing to say of her past business association
with his wife Mary. Even former employee Pat Key
grudgingly admitted he had a style and could look quite
dapper. Practically the only person who consistently said
anything good about Dennis Hill was former nanny
Deane David, who has had her own critics.

David Long, who owns the Shell service station in Heathrow—it was an Exxon station at the time of the fatal crash—said Dennis Hill was a nice man, who had traded at this business for a long time. Administrators at the family's church in Longwood remember the whole family as being very nice.

Can one person have such a diametrically opposed personality, that his deeds can be perceived by some as pure goodness and by others as something far less than goodness? It is hard to believe some things said about him concerning his sexual conduct, when you consider his obvious pain and grief over the death of his daughter. Even Jennifer, his stepdaughter, who had reason to be critical of his treatment of her mother, her sister and herself, found admirable things to say about Dennis Hill. She admired his business sense and drive.

How did things reach this state? Dennis Hill must have had many good points and characteristics to have achieved the fantastic success he had in business. He was a self-made man.

If "central casting" sent out a call for a "James Cagney type," Dennis Hill would immediately be hired. A man of average height and looks, with dark brownish red hair and brown eyes, you immediately have the impression of him that he could be a formidable foe, in business or anything else. He exudes a pugnacious quality, which is difficult to ignore. Film clips and photos of him when he was smiling and dressed in a tuxedo give the impression of a confident, socially adept man. *Who* and *what* is Dennis Hill?

Former employees and family members, including his wife Mary Hill, have accused the man of perverse deeds, of being a womanizer, doing things and exhibiting behavior unacceptable to most of society. It is true, most people have secrets they think will never become public knowledge, but most people don't find themselves at the center of a high-profile felony case *and* divorce case *and* child custody case that garner the attention of the national media. There comes a time when no secrets are held sacred, especially in a divorce case.

Dennis Hill seemed to relish the prospect of the coming fight when he told *48 Hours* reporter Peter Van Sant that *The War of the Roses,* referring to a movie about a divorcing couple, would be nothing compared to *The War of the Hills.* He even told him that no one would believe it—even if they followed the Hills around and filmed the whole thing.

What was known about him was that he could use very rough language at the drop of a hat; yet he could sit down at a piano and coax beautiful music from the keys.

One of the things that nanny Deane David found admirable was his generosity and his love and attention to his daughters Amy and Kaitlynn.

In a deposition for the Browns' and Rockwells' civil suits against the Hills, David was very supportive of Dennis Hill. She told attorneys John Morgan and Thomas Neal that Dennis originally purchased the Barbara Nolan agency for Mary, to give her something to do. Increasingly, however, he found himself running it more and more, and not going to Chicago. Because he didn't know how Mary was going to be, from one minute to the next, "he stayed home a lot for the kids," David said.

She was critical of Mary Hill in her treatment of Dennis, saying Mary just couldn't move past Dennis's infidelity and fathering a son outside of their marriage. According to David, Mary would constantly call the boy the "little bastard child," even in front of the girls, and was hypercritical of Dennis to them. "We talked about that (the child issue) . . . and it was like, you know, we all make choices here. You know, are you going to let it kill you or are you going to, you know, move on with your life?"

David said Amy would tell her the family was dysfunctional and David had to agree with her. When Morgan and Neal asked why, she told them, "Because any one outstanding person in the house that conducts themselves in the manner that Mary did, and that was—I mean, she would never do anything for the children. She never picked them up. She never took them to dance. I mean, this was all up to me and Dennis. And she would complain about 'Dennis never did anything.' And I'm like, you know, how much do you want from him? In my thoughts, I didn't say it, of course. I mean, how much do you want him to do, and me?"

David said she was also put off by the "extreme amount of disrespect" that Amy and Kaitlynn had for their father, no matter how he tried. "And the girls would always come to me and they would bad-mouth him, and say, 'Well, you know, my mom says that . . . '; so, I hear it coming that Mary's bad-mouthing Dennis . . . about everything . . . about the infidelity issue. I mean, these girls knew this."

David said the girls received many mixed signals from their parents. "Mary made a lot of promises that she never kept. And Dennis would always try so hard. And I know the girls loved him, and they did show affection with Dennis, you know, many times."

When asked if the girls showed affection toward Mary, David said they wanted to, but felt shut out. "Mary [was] always like 'I'm in my room,' and she just didn't want to be bothered."

When asked about Dennis's friends, she admitted she had not met many. "Mostly friends from Chicago would call from time to time," she said.

"I only met one couple, a couple of couples. There was a man, John, I can't remember his last name," she said. He was in real estate, and helped Dennis with the eulogy for Amy.

"Nobody" was David's reply when she was asked who called the house to speak to Mary. She shook her head no when asked if Mary had any friends. She recalled a big Christmas party the Hills gave, where there were a lot people in attendance, but she said not many people called the house that she knew of.

David said Dennis Hill's older children came for Thanksgiving while she was employed there. She got to know his daughters Heather and Julie quite well. "They couldn't stand Mary. They were so upset and had been for many, many years with Mary and her attitude," Dean said.

They didn't like "her attitude, the way they treated her, the way she treated their father. They knew that she was doing drugs; they knew that she was taking a lot of painkillers."

She admitted to David she was addicted to them. She later told David not to worry about the addictions, as she had a "handle on things."

"'Don't worry about me,' she says. 'You should have seen me when Dennis went through the infidelity situation,' she goes, 'I was falling apart.' She was like manic-depressive, on a lot of downers. 'I'm nothing compared to what I was, you know. If you're worried about the cocaine,' she goes, 'it's not like I do that every day. I'll tell you right now, I'm addicted to painkillers.' But she didn't say, 'I'm not addicted to cocaine.'"

David said many times she wanted to tell Dennis about the cocaine use, but couldn't without betraying Mary's confidence. "Dennis knew that I knew that she was off her rocker, because of her behavior. I mean, I never knew what Mary expected from me, from one minute to the next. I mean, I could be ready to walk out the door and she would want me to prepare an entire meal for somebody at the office, you know, for an office party. Just yanking, you know, just yanking stuff.

"But I didn't get too frustrated because I knew she was sick. Dennis and I would just kind of roll our eyes in the back of our heads. His weakness came with the fact that he just dealt with it, because he had several businesses to run and was trying to keep up with the girls.

"He would just get to a point where I think it was a weakness. Instead of putting his foot down and doing something about any of it. We just kind of all rolled our eyes in our head. It was like an expectation of knowing that Mary was just the way she was, the queen bee."

David said she first addressed Mary's drug use and behavior while they were preparing for Christmas and the big Christmas party. They were all trying to get it together, doing the food and everything else. "Dennis was at his wit's end," said David. "And I just [said], 'Dennis, she needs help.' He goes, 'No shit.'

"No shit," that's what he said, David recalled. "I said, I'm getting worried about the girls at this point. And he assured me, at that point in time, that those girls were not getting in the car with her, they were not doing anything with her; he was adamant about that."

Dennis Hill said those worries were why he went and picked the girls up and would take them to things when David wasn't around. David said she thought he was so adamant about it because "he knew that she was on drugs, because we talked about it." David claimed she never broke her confidence with Mary, but did tell Dennis, "She's got a problem here and we're not just talking—okay, we're not just talking about your average painkiller here, Dennis." She described Dennis as being "a little panicky" upon receiving this news. "See, Jennifer had already tried to tell him. And I don't think that he disbelieved us, I think that he didn't want to believe that she was that far into it. And he was just . . . he was scared. I know he was scared." David told him the solution was rehab. She said he totally agreed with her.

David said she told Dennis about an episode of Mary and Amy having a really bad fight, and Mary speeding recklessly out of the garage and down the drive. When he came home from work, she told him, "Man, I don't like this."

David said when she first began working for the Hills, Dennis would fly out of town once in a while. "He'd be gone for, like, a week at a time. And he just got to where he couldn't trust leaving Mary with the kids alone, so he started staying home more."

David said she could see Mary's downward spiral after Christmas and finally quit in February 2000. "I started to feel beat up and Dennis knew it. I mean, even the kids knew it, everybody knew it. I mean, it's one thing to be hired to work in the house; it's another thing to have to live someone else's life. I told Dennis, you know, I can work for you, but I can't live her life for her. And he understood. And I needed a pay raise."

The attorneys asked her if she asked for one, and she said, "Oh, absolutely, I did ask for that. . . . It wasn't up to Dennis, it was all up to Mary. And it was offensive when you see somebody buying, you know, jewelry like crazy and oriental rugs. I mean, impulsive buying—and then [they] tell you, there's just no way they could pay you any more money than they're paying you. It was my excuse to find something else to move on."

David said she was getting attached to the girls, and she was being affected by seeing what they were going through. And the many fights between Mary and Dennis were affecting her as well. She witnessed "more annoyance between the two of them than anything." But she said the girls would "come to me all the time," with stories about the fights. "It took a lot for Dennis to explode, but he did. He would have a temper when the occasion arose."

David said, "They were always in turmoil about their mom and dad." David said about the time Jennifer approached Dennis about her mom's cocaine use, they were going to separate.

David said she and Dennis had a conversation shortly before she gave the deposition, and they both were totally surprised at the fact that no drugs were found in Mary's system after the crash. "Both of us were, you know, kind of amazed."

Dennis Hill participated in a deposition himself, conducted by state prosecutor Pat Whitaker and Ted Culhane's team of defense attorneys. He was very forthcoming on a number of subjects, down to admitting that he didn't always know what plans his children were concocting. On the subject of picking the kids up from school, he said it was a very informal thing, and all the kids would just get in the car, there never was any question of leaving any one of the three—Amy, Carrie or Zak—behind.

He described Amy as a "Mary-clone."

"I think they are fairly close," he said. He said Amy was very smart and he felt that Amy and his wife had a good relationship.

"Okay. A lot of times, kids go into adolescence, get rebellious, and so forth, and can push buttons. They know how to push the buttons on their parents. Amy was no different," he said, from any other normal thirteen-year-old. "She was very bright and she knew what buttons to push. But Mary was able to take her button pushing a lot better than I could.

"Amy was just starting to enter that part, you know, being a teen." He described his daughter as "a very mature kid. She and Mary got along because she liked to go shopping with Mary and feeling that element of being older. Which, you know, she was only thirteen, but she was aspiring to be a seventeen-year-old the next day."

The only conflicts Dennis Hill could recall that he had with Amy, if anything, would be his objection to the amount of makeup she wore in the mornings. "She was just a real easy child to raise."

Dennis said he couldn't even remember the day of the crash anymore. He vaguely recalled driving before a trooper, probably a sheriff's deputy, showing him where the Rockwells and Browns lived in Wingfield North. The only outstanding thing he remembered, other than wanting to be wrong about Amy and Carrie's deaths, was getting into a discussion with the emergency/rescue person in charge at the scene. Hill wanted to stay until Amy and Carrie were removed from the wreckage, and the medic opposed it. Mel Stevens, who was nearly arrested at the scene, until someone recognized him and said he could stay, did stay on the scene as workers held up a blue tarp while the girls' bodies were removed from Mary Hill's BMW.

Dennis Hill has said no one should put any credence in anything he said that day, as he was so distraught. Today he remembers little of what he said.

Hill said when he first came upon the wreck, he did recall saying to himself, "'Jesus, look at that. Some crazy guy tore his car up.' It was my car. So, when I stopped, the only thing I really remember distinctly [was] just running and the two guys standing there, and I said, 'Somebody call nine-one-one,' and they said 'I don't have a phone.' I had my phone and I was trying to call nine-one-one. I was trying to get in the backseat with the girls. Zak [had a] very strong pulse. Carrie had none and Amy had none. I tried femur pulse. I tried carotid pulse. I tried everything and there was just nothing."

When Dennis was quizzed about the status of his marriage, he said it had no more than the normal bumps. When it was countered with "What is normal?" He agreed, saying, "Yeah, Well, that's true.

"Did I sleep with my wife every night? Yes," he said. "Did we not speak? No. Did we argue about different things? Yes. Nobody slugged each other," he said. He said they weren't the Cleavers (actually, he said the Beavers). He said he did not ask his wife for a divorce on the day of the crash, despite rumors flying around that he did. He admitted he had fathered a child outside of their marriage, saying it was a long time ago. He said "everything" about their relationship "was aboveboard till that whole disaster."

He did deny knowing Mary abused drugs. "She had a substance abuse problem? I was not aware."

He admitted, "It's true you start dissecting anybody's

marriage, you'll come up with the rocks, but no, it (their marriage) was pretty good. It was pretty good."

He said he didn't want Mary charged for the crash. "Because the woman is consumed with so much grief and guilt, there's nothing anybody could do to make it worse, absolutely nothing. And I understand why people cut and run when things like this happen. I know that nine out of ten marriages end when a child is lost, and I understand that. But my wife has stood by me in the past, I'll stand by her. But there's nobody who suffers more every day than her. It's beyond . . . I have no idea how she suffers. The grief is just overwhelming, and the guilt is staggering."

When asked if he thought she would ever get over it, he said, "I don't think so. I don't think so."

His answer was "Amen" was when he was asked if he was being sued. He thought there were three different lawsuits, but wasn't quite sure if the Brown family's suit had been combined into one. "Well, there's the Browns' lawsuit. Now, there's a splinter off of that, and I'm not quite sure. See, Carrie's mother and father were divorced. Her father lives in Minneapolis, and it's money driven. So, now all of a sudden, he wants to know how much am I gonna get? I tell you, I want to shoot these people. And I don't know if that's the third one that was filed. The Rockwells filed and then the Rita Brown suit. And the reason I said three, because I thought the Rita Brown [suit] was splintered, but maybe they got together. I don't know."

Dennis expressed his concern and love for daughter Kaitlynn and what she was going through. He said she missed her mom because Mary was just grieving all the time. He said, "She just looks at you and she says, 'Well, if Amy's in heaven and in a better place, I'm sorry, why is Mom so sad?' And I said, she misses her a lot.

"And I said, 'Kaitlynn, I miss her a lot, too, I'm just a little bit stronger than Mom. So that means, I'm gonna have to help you. So we're gonna have to let Mom get well.' And that's what hurts. Because she really can't function, helping with Kaitlynn, because she's so zeroed in on Amy and carrying the guilt and that whole thing. It's just slowly . . . she's just dying on me, and they won't do anything, they can't do anything."

Hill's insurance finally settled the civil suits, paying the Browns $2 million and the Rockwells $1 million, the total being the limit of the insurance.

Angel or devil? There's some of both in most people . . . and few can likely stand up to the intense scrutiny *everyone* involved in this case has undergone.

CHAPTER 11

Luckier than one's neighbor,
but still not happy.

—Euripides

One of the most controversial figures to come forward in the Mary Hill case, was former nanny Deane David. She worked for Mary Hill in the capacity of a nanny for six months, leaving her service over a pay dispute in February 2000, six months before the crash occurred. She said she quit. Mary Hill, in court testimony, said she fired her. The two of them were likely the only two people who did know what transpired in the termination of their relationship, or which one terminated it.

David somewhat resembles a shorter version of the entertainer Cher when she first became well-known. She has dark brown hair, with very long brown bangs, which come down to, and frame, warm brownish eyes. It looks as though it is a hairstyle she has worn since the 1970s—a little "hippie" but not too extreme. She is a chatty person with a personality best described as very friendly. She's the comfortable type of woman you could meet, sit down for coffee with, and tell her your life's story, without even realizing it— and you could find out hers as well. Although not a professional nanny, she had the type of charm that could easily win the confidence of a child.

Prior to accepting the position in the Hill household, David had been married to a very wealthy man, who had become rich after developing a computer/photo technique. After going through the divorce, she was looking for a better job to support her family. She was interested when she found a notice for a nanny job. She contacted Doris Scott at Barbara Nolan, who was screening applicants, and was told her employer was looking for someone like "an Alice from *The Brady Bunch.*"

I can do that, she told herself. After all, she had been doing just that for years for her own family. After being interviewed by both Doris Scott and Dennis Hill, she was told final approval was up to Mary Hill. She was sent over to the Wingfield North house for an interview. She jumped at the opportunity when Mary explained what her duties would be, and asked her if "eight" sounded okay to her for pay? That offer of "eight" became a point of contention between the two women. David apparently thought $800 a week and Hill $8 an hour. David accepted the position. "I was chief cook and bottle washer," she told attorneys in a deposition. "I was living their lives, and not my own." In the end, she decided she had to leave; the pay also remained a major issue.

The strongest feeling that came across from her depositions, trial testimony and in personal conversation was that she really felt compassion for the Hill family and what they were going through. She quickly bonded with the girls, Amy and Kaitlynn. She seemed to have been motivated by that bond, to stay with the family, as long as she could, despite her need to earn more money and have more time with her own family—and despite the growing conflict with her employer Mary Hill. Personal conflict between them continued after she left Hill's household.

At times, some of her deposed testimony seemed to be in conflict with previous testimony, but it was difficult to recall details on demand—for events, down to minute detail, that happened a few years before. The basic narrative of her testimonies seemed to agree, although differing slightly in some small details, here and there. Whether or not she had mixed up names, dates and some anecdotal stories over time, her general memories offer insight into the Hills' family life, a place where few outsiders had been allowed.

Deane now works as a sales associate for a pavement-restoration business. She has worked for it since leaving Hills' employ. She recalled her past employment experience with the Hills in a deposition conducted by Tim Berry, Mary Hill's defense attorney, and prosecuting attorney Pat Whitaker, prior to the trial. "Everything" was her reply to Berry's question about her duties in the Hill household. "I cleaned, I cooked the meals, picked up the kids from school, took the kids to dance lessons or piano lessons. I washed the clothes. I did the grocery shopping. I picked up. I helped Mary with her mother from time to time when she was there, if I had to get prescriptions or whatever.

"I guess it would be, what didn't I do, would be more the question, because I think I just did about everything a person could possibly do."

David said she had equal contact with both Dennis and Mary Hill. She recalled that "Mary was in her room most of the time when I was working. But we did interact. When Mary went to work, when Dennis would come home while I was cooking. Then Dennis and I would interact . . . mainly with Dennis, it was dinnertime."

After leaving the Hills, the first time David talked with Mary Hill—after the accident—was when she called the house from her office to see if she could reach Kaitlynn. "Mary picked up the phone, and at first she was very upset with me, but then she rolled into wanting to talk about Amy. Then she discussed with me, that she still cannot remember what happened.

"She was upset with me, because she felt that I had enough information to put her away for thirty years, that's what she told me. I told her that was not my intent. My intent was just to tell the truth of what I knew."

Berry was curious as to what she knew that would result in this. "What is this information that she believes you have that is harmful?" he asked.

"The fact that I knew that she was doing cocaine, two weeks into the job," said David. "It had fallen out of her purse. Her mother had asked me if I would pick her purse up, because she was in a walker and she couldn't bend over and pick it up. I found the compact and the cocaine and the razor blade and the whole—"

"How did you know that was cocaine?" Berry asked.

"I took it and licked it. It's chemical tasting, numbs you up."

"Had you ever tasted cocaine before?"

"Yes, I have," she replied.

"When was that?"

"Oh, I don't know," Deane David said. "Years ago, back in the '70s. I was always too afraid to actually do it, but I have tasted it, yes."

When Berry asked her if she had used any other drugs, she admitted that back in the 1970s, as a kid, she had smoked pot.

Berry was still interested in what she could possibly know about Mary Hill that would have such a devastating effect on her freedom. "What other information do you feel you have, that would put her away for thirty years?" he asked.

"Incidents that happened in the home," she said. "Incidents that happened when she was angry with Amy when they were going to the mall and she screeched out of the garage and squealed out of the driveway, almost hitting the two fences, with Kaitlynn in the car."

One of the main events she recalled was a time when she was cooking dinner. Amy, Kaitlynn and Mary were going to the mall, but someone, she thought it was Mary—it was Kaitlynn or Mary—didn't want to go. She recalled Amy saying, "'You promised you would take us.'

"It was one of those just-mom-and-daughter things, and they ended up getting in the car. Next thing I know, Amy comes running in [from] the garage, screaming and crying her eyes out, because her and Mary had a knock-down-drag-out in the garage."

David didn't see the argument, but "witnessed Amy coming in the house hysterical. What I did witness is that I was so upset at her being that upset that I walked out to the garage—at the time, Mary and Kaitlynn—with Kaitlynn's eyes being absolutely like an owl, scared out of her mind, that Mary was screeching out of the back of the driveway. And then I followed into the garage and watched her tear down out of the driveway, almost hitting the"—she paused—

"almost hitting the gate or the columns, and tearing down the street.

"It was late afternoon, probably around five." David usually left around 6:00 P.M.

When she was deposed for the civil suit, soon after the crash, David would say Mary Hill usually got up around 11:00 A.M. to noon. She would stay in the back bedroom until she actually came out to go to work, anywhere between 2:00 to 4:00 P.M. She worked later than Dennis, and he would come home about the time Kaitlynn got home from school, David recalled. She said he found himself running Barbara Nolan more and more, and not going to Chicago as frequently.

"He had an office there (Barbara Nolan) and also an office in the home. Then he would fly off to wherever, you know, to Chicago, and [then] for his other companies."

When David was there, a typical day in the household started for her at 10:00 A.M. when she arrived at work. The kids would have left already for school. She thought that Amy took the school bus in the morning, and that Dennis usually took Kaitlynn and dropped her off at Heathrow Elementary on his way to work when he was in town. Kaitlynn took the bus home every day. David would meet her at the bus stop.

When she arrived for work, "I just started in . . . whatever needed to get done." Occasionally she would have to go into Mary's bedroom to see her, but usually not. Mary would just come out dressed, and ready to go to work, just before Kaitlynn got home, around 2:45 P.M., according to David.

Describing her reclusive employer's morning schedule, David said, "She was just taking her time, you know, or sleeping, or putting her makeup on, or getting ready. I've never seen a woman take so long to get ready. . . . I've never seen a woman take so ong to get dressed, in my whole life. I mean, it was kind of a family joke about the situation. Life did not begin for Mary until, you know, two-thirty in the afternoon.

"As far as I know, she was dressed to go. That's where the kids—once in a while—would get a hold of her at work. So, I know she was there. If she had other stops or whatever," David didn't know, "but she was always dressed to walk out to go to work."

David described to Berry and Whitaker another incident when "we were all putting the Christmas decorations together, and everybody was feeling very concerned for Mary at this point, because she was basically hiding in her room most of the time, which she did a lot, anyway. This is more than ever.

"She was having everybody hiring all these people to come in and do all these decorations. And it was at that point that I remember just being worried, you know. I talked to her assistant and I said, 'I'm really worried about Mary, okay? I think she needs some help.' And that's all I said to her.

"She went into Mary and, I guess, kind of blew it out of proportion, like I said she needed to be Baker Acted or, you know, put in a facility. And that's not what I said to her." David confronted the employee in front of Hill, to set the record straight, that she did not say Hill should be placed under enforced mental observation in a hospital, or Baker Acted.

"Mary came out to me in tears and she says, 'If Dennis finds out anything about anything,' she goes, 'I will lose my children.' And I said 'Mary, I work for you. It's not my place to be in your business.' I go, however, 'I do work for you and I am concerned for you.'"

David and Mary talked with the assistant, and David said she pointed out to both of them that she only said Mary needed help. "So, that was an incident, you know, because Mary was very distraught that she would lose her children, because if Dennis found out she was doing cocaine.

"She called me up and asked me not to come to work one morning, because I guess her and Jennifer, her oldest daughter, had gotten in an argument. And she said, 'I need to get them out of the house, so don't come to work today.' And, you know, 'I'll talk to you about it.' She called me back up and she says, 'Are you believing that Jennifer is trying to tell Dennis that I'm doing cocaine?'

"Well, see, I already knew at this point that she was. And, I just said, 'Well, Mary, you know, call me if you need help.' I didn't make any comment to what she said to me. I just said, 'Call me and let me know if you need some help with the kids.'

"She said, 'Well, Amy is going to stay over at Rita's.' And, Kaitlynn, I think was going to stay over at Vicki Hartzell's. And, I go, 'All right.'

"So, then I went the next day to work, called back in, and Amy basically cornered me. This is tough for me right here. This is the tough part. And she said to me, 'Do you think my mother is doing drugs?'

"And I said, 'Amy,' I said, 'no matter what happens,' I said, 'none of this is you and Kaitlynn's fault.' I said, 'You're a very strong girl.' And I said, 'You can come and talk to me anytime.' And I said, 'Do you think . . .' I said, 'It's not a question of whether I think your mother is doing drugs or not.' I said, 'If you think she is, and you think your family needs to pull together, and you think you need to help your mom in any way,' I go, 'that's a decision for you and your family to make. But I'm not here to pass judgment.' And I said, 'I don't know.'

"I mean, I knew she was doing drugs, but I wasn't going to tell her, a twelve-year-old child, that she was. I was just helping her handle the pain of what she had heard that was going on with Jennifer and Mary."

On the day David didn't go into work, Jennifer and her family left the household. "Mary kicked them out. . . . I guess Mary kicked out Jennifer and her husband and the baby. She was staying in the pool house over there across from the pool. I remember Jennifer coming in at one point to get some of her stuff. It wasn't the next day, but I think a couple of days after that, just shaking her head. She looked at me and she goes, 'I don't know what else to do.' She goes, 'You know, Dennis isn't going to listen to me.' She goes, 'I'm worried about her picking the kids up from school or doing anything in the car with them.' And she goes, 'I really don't know what to do.' And she goes, 'I know you're in a position where you can't do anything because you work here.'

"And it just scared the daylights out of me and Jennifer that one day something like what happened was going to happen."

Berry asked David if she could relate events she was aware of regarding Hill's behavior. David said there were—one was Mary Hill's frustration with Kaitlynn.

"I think her temper with Kaitlynn [was a problem]. She would get frustrated with Kaitlynn. Kaitlynn would come home from school and Kaitlynn would want her attention. And Mary would always, you know, try to avoid or get out of the house before Kaitlynn came home, so she wouldn't have to, you know, deal with Kaitlynn when she came home.

"I was always put in a position with Mary that if

Dennis called and Dennis would go, 'Where is she at? She's supposed to be here.' Mary would go, 'Tell Dennis I'm on my way,' or 'Tell Dennis something, but don't tell him I'm here.'

"And I always felt I was in the middle, because I felt like I had to lie for Mary. And that was very uncomfortable for me. There were incidents like that where there was always, you know, some arguing between the two of them of where Mary was at.

"Mary would come flying into the kitchen sometimes, with no makeup and hair [*sic*], and say, 'I've got to go, I've got to go,' and she would run off and be gone and not come home until wee hours of the night, so the kids would tell me.

"The next incident is when I left. That stands out in my mind. When Amy called me up and she said, 'I just wanted to let you know that Mom has checked herself into La Amistad' (a drug rehabilitation clinic).

"And I said, 'Well, praise God, Amy.' I go, 'Maybe this is the beginning of the end of the problems that you're having to deal with.' And she said, 'Yeah, I'm really happy about it that she's there.' I go, 'Well, great,' I go, 'Listen, ask your dad if it's all right with your dad that I could pick you up from school.' I hadn't seen them in several months." Later, Amy called David back, saying her dad said it would be okay for her to pick up Amy at school the next day, so they could see each other.

"That was the last time I saw Amy—when I went to go pick her up from school. And I brought my son Michael with me, because he liked Amy a lot, too. And I got to visit with her a little bit. I guess it was about a week later and I called the house. Mary answered the phone, and I said, 'Oh!' I said, 'What are you doing there?' She goes, 'Well, what do mean what am I doing here?'

"I go, 'Amy called and told me that you had, you know, gone into La Amistad, and they were really happy that, you know . . . I hope you're feeling good.'

"She goes, 'I never want you to lay your eyes or ever come over to my house or ever see my children again.' And she slammed down the phone. And I had to honor that, because that's their mother, and she said I couldn't see them. So, that's the last time I saw or talked to Amy." She said she decided not to make trouble by calling Dennis and telling him what happened.

"Basically, I was only making three-hundred a week for doing everything that I was doing, and I really could not afford to stay there. Plus, it was getting so dysfunctional there, that I was—it was like I felt like I was spending more time with this family than I was with my own. I lived over in Metro West (outside of Orlando in Orange County). I was trying to take care of this family and these girls, you know, far away. You know, she was having me sometimes stay a little later, and do a lot of different things, you know, that were not in the scope of work that I was hired [to do].

"So, it got to the point where I couldn't survive on three hundred a week. And I knew that I took"—she paused—"when I took the job, I took it with a note that I would be making more money later on down the line with more responsibilities."

At first, David was told, "that I would be taking the kids. That I would be helping Kaitlynn when she got home with her schoolwork. I would be cooking dinner and cleaning the house."

As with so much discontent that seemed to occur with Mary Hill's employees, money was part of the problem. "The financial arrangement at the very beginning," said David, "I thought she said, 'Is eight okay?' I said that's fine.

"So when I started working, I thought she meant eight hundred a week. Because I mean, I was doing a lot of work. And she said, 'Oh, no. No, my God. I can't give you [that].' I mean, I understand three hundred a week if somebody is going to come in and clean your house. But she said eight hundred. And I said, 'Oh, God,' and I [had] already started. I didn't want to leave the girls. I already made a commitment.

"I said, 'All right, I'll stay.' I didn't have a lot of overhead. Okay, let's see if this works. I said, 'Well, I can do it, you know, for however long I can do it, until I can't do it any more financially.'

"So things just got so bad. I never knew where her moods were going to be—it was like a downward spiral. And I just felt . . . I just felt it was time to go."

David said she was there for only a short time, but she wanted everyone to know the truth "from the short time that I was there, from me."

David recalled that on a whim she called the Hill home sometime after the crash, probably in September or October. The children had been on her mind and she was hoping Kaitlynn would pick up the phone. Mary Hill, answered, instead. That was when Mary told David that she had the information to put her, Mary, away for thirty years.

David told her "that wasn't my intent." Hill didn't hang up the phone, and it seemed to David, she really wanted to talk to her. "I'm up against a situation where I have to tell the truth about what I know," David told Hill. "You know how much I loved Amy and Kaitlynn. She went on to tell me, 'You know that I can't believe, you know, what happened. I still can't remember what, you know, after the accident.'

"'Mary, do you not remember anything?'" David asked. "She said, 'Well, I'm really not even supposed to be talking to you. But I can't remember anything.' She really wanted to talk with me about Amy, because she knew that Amy and I were close. I told her that I'd seen Amy in a dream and she's doing fine—because she knows I'm Christian.

"Mary really didn't want to have anything to do with God after her father died. It was kind of a thing for her. So I didn't press that with her. That was the way she felt. But I did tell her that if she prays and asked Jesus to bring Amy into her dreams, he'll do that for her.

"I said, 'She's fine,' and she wanted to hear it. She wanted to hear me tell my dream. And we had, it was a nice conversation.

"She said, 'I really can't talk to you on the phone. I can't talk anymore.' So, she had to hang up. I said, 'I understand.'"

David called the Hill home again to speak to Kaitlynn, a month or two after that conversation—the timeline was a little hazy to her. Mary Hill picked up the phone again. "She said, 'Oh, did you hear that Julie lost her baby?' That's the first thing she said to me. Like how was I supposed to know what happened to Julie? I've been so away from this family—that how would I even know? Julie lives up in, I think, Chicago.

"I said, 'No. What happened to Julie?' I knew that Julie was pregnant when Amy died. When I went over to the funeral and I spoke with Julie, she said that she was pregnant again.

"Mary said to me, 'Well, Julie lost the baby.' When

I say, 'Oh, that's horrible,' she goes, 'Well, I don't think it's horrible.' She goes, 'I'm glad. You know she was such a bitch to me through this whole thing with Amy and being like this with me. I'm really glad that she's got a taste of what it feels like.' At that point, I was like, 'Whoa. Okay, we're not learning anything from this, are we, Mary?' I mean, I didn't say that. But in my mind, I'm going, we're not. Somewhere, we're not getting the fact that you're alive and you've got an opportunity here to make things right. She just totally turned the tables and said that. I just went, 'Well, sorry to hear that.'

"I don't even remember the rest [of the conversation]. When you hear something like that, it just kind of throws you off a little bit. I don't even remember [what else was said]. That's God's honest truth. There wasn't a whole lot I could say to Mary after hearing something like that. Because I was close to Julie and I was close to Heather and I was close to all Dennis's kids when they came down. You know, I cooked for them. I was more close with Heather. In that six-month time frame, I had a relationship with these people. So, to hear something like that pretty much blocks out anything else that was said.

"At the very beginning, when I first . . . of course, when I first heard about it (the crash), it was like something threw a brick at my head. So, when I made it to the house, I think I talked to Dennis on that afternoon or the next day.

"I found out standing in a Mobil station. It was everything I could do to get out of that station— when I'm looking at her and Carrie's face on the front-page news. So I never got to see Amy again after that day [that I picked her up at school].

"He just says, 'My God, Deane, I just don't understand

this. I let her pick them up from the school. Amy was in-
sisting that her mother pick her up from school because
she promised. She didn't want to ride the bus, it was the
first day of school and she promised. Mary said, "I
promised Amy I would pick her up from school.'"

"'Drop me off at the gas station,'" David recounted
Dennis Hill said. "'Then the next thing I knew, five
minutes later, I'm walking into Amy being dead and
this horrible nightmare.'

"He just was frantic, you know. He just . . . it was
almost like he knew, you know, we both all knew we
didn't want her to pick the kids up from school,
based on her behavior. She has an anger management
situation; she's doing drugs. You never know when
she's going to flip out or not. I mean, she had zero
tolerance, zero tolerance with the children. It was one
of the reasons why she stayed in her room a lot."

The next time David saw any of the Hill family was
at the service for Amy. Jennifer came up to her, she
recalled, and they both burst into tears at the same
time. Jennifer gave her a big hug, said David, and told
her, "'We knew this was going to happen.'

"We knew this was going to happen," David said.
"We were devastated. There was nothing we could do
to stop it."

David went up to Mary Hill, who was in a wheelchair
at the funeral, to share her feelings of sympathy with
her, for a mother who had lost her child. She remembered there were a few tears and not much
about the interchange. "Her demeanor afterward
kind of concerned me," David said of Hill's behavior
after the service was over. "It was cavalier. We all went
over to the house, but Mary never said two words to
me over at the house.

"I was equally close to both of them (Amy and

Kaitlynn), just in a different way. They're different ages. They're both very, very different.

"The only incident I know (after her departure from the Hill employ) is that not from when I was working there, I just know from when I talked to Kaitlynn. I had found out she was living with Jennifer. We only had two conversations and we had an agreement that I would not contact her, we would not be in touch with each other until after the trial.

"Kaitlynn was so upset, she couldn't see straight when she heard my voice, because I hadn't seen her in a long time, and she was so upset [about] the fact that she said her mom tried to kill her, driving the car down the street going to dance lessons—and told her that it should have been her (Kaitlynn) and not Amy (that was killed). Kaitlynn said she was screaming, telling her mom to stop the car. 'Please stop the car, Mom.' She said her mom was basically hysterical in the car.

"I don't know when this happened. She just told me it did happen. She also pointed out to me, her mom and them were divorcing, and that there was just a nightmare going on between them. Allegations about . . . I guess her mom stating that her dad was trying—was abusing her and all this crazy stuff that was going on, you know, within the family. My heart was sick for her. I was trying to be encouraging by telling her that I was very happy that she was with Jennifer, because Jennifer has always been her favorite sibling. She has always been close to Jennifer. Jennifer was the one that always gave Kaitlynn a lot of attention. I was happy that she was safe and that she was there."

David remembered telling her, "One day, we were all going to get past this. And that I looked forward to spending some time with her when it's all over and said and done."

David remembered Kaitlynn telling her about another ride with her mother. "She said the one incident that really was the icing on the cake, that she said she couldn't take it anymore, was when she was taking her to dance class and she was going seventy miles an hour, scaring the hell out of her. Obviously she was still with Mary, but I don't know where Dennis was—if they were separated or not. But I know Mary was driving her.

"Last time I talked [to] and saw Dennis (before the crash) is when I picked Amy up from school and we talked a little bit in the kitchen and I said, 'Well, I'm glad she's made the decision to go into, you know, [La Amistad]. He goes, 'I had nothing to do with it. She did it on her own.' I go, 'that's the best part.' A week later, she's back in the house again. That was [one of] the last times I talked to Dennis."

David recalled in the conversation that she had with Mary—when Mary had said she couldn't remember what happened in the crash—that she didn't remember what happened afterward: "All she remembers is sliding on gravel. She said to me, 'All I remember is sliding on the rocks; then I don't remember anything after that.' I'm like what rocks? There isn't any rocks over there."

David had her own theory about what may have happened, which she shared with the attorneys present at the deposition. She thought she knew what happened "because I know the kids in the backseat of the car.

"She (Mary) just kept saying, she doesn't remember. She doesn't remember.

"I'm having a comeback here," she said, suddenly

remembering a past conversation. "Kaitlynn told me at the beginning of the accident that she said that her mother told her in the hospital that all she did was turn back to say something to Amy, and she didn't remember anything after that. That's what Kaitlynn told me, that Mary told Kaitlynn. That's all she did, was turn back to look—you know.

"And, I'm thinking, well, the only reason why you would do that is if you're angry, and instead of looking through the rearview mirror when you're mad, because she's very impulsive with her temper. I can see her jerking back. And, you know, smacking her (Amy) or swinging or whatever.

"But I do remember Kaitlynn saying, 'My mom said to me, when she was in the hospital, all she did was turn back and look. . . .' This was right after the accident. I'm trying to remember if it was over the phone. It had to be over the phone. About the time I was talking to Dennis over the phone after—right after the car accident. When I was talking to Jennifer about it, I go, you know, Kaitlynn is saying, you know, Mary turned around. She says, 'Yeah.' She goes, 'That's what she said.'"

But David also attributed this information to Mary Hill's stepdaughter Heather in an earlier deposition, which was closer in time to the crash, saying, "Heather told me that Mary had called Kaitlynn in the hospital to tell her, 'I'm sorry Kaitlynn. All Mommy did was turn around to say something to Amy and Carrie.' You know Carrie could be very hyper, and then that would bring it out in Amy, so both of them would pop the music up too loud or something. All we can figure is maybe Mary just, you know, maybe either lost her temper, or my first thing is, she's turning around to tell them to be quiet, instead of looking in the rear-view mirror at them.

"The only thing I remember Jennifer telling me was that she was at the hospital and really upset with Mary, because all she was worried about was her jewelry. You know. And that's where Jennifer's real upset was coming from, because she couldn't figure out why, you know, she was so concerned about her jewelry."

CHAPTER 12

Truth is always strange, stranger than fiction.
                                              —Lord Byron

There never was any dispute about *what* happened on August 7, 2000, when Mary Hill, at the steering wheel of her BMW, sped down Markham Woods Road, her car going out of control, colliding with a substantial live oak, killing two people and injuring two others. The question has always been: *why* did it happen? Was an out-of-control woman driving so recklessly, she was bound to kill or injure someone? Or was she, and her passengers, the helpless victims of a car that went out of control, speeding down the road on its own, carrying two people to their deaths, injuring two others? Were they all victims of a heartless, merciless, metal machine, not governed by heart, mind or soul? Or were they victims of a woman who bragged to employees about her constant speeding, who frightened passengers riding in her car with her recklessness and rages, culminating in excessive speeds—a lethal combination on the roadway. Mary Hill has a heart, a mind and a soul, but in her car, did she listen to them, or did she wield her car, like a weapon, to act out fits of rage, regardless of the harm she was bound to cause someday?

In the forty-three months between the time when the crash occurred and when the trial began, there was an incredible amount of media coverage about the case. Both local print and local television followed the story—then the CBS feature news show, *48 Hours,* entered the picture. According to a senior press representative for the show, they have producers constantly reading publications and watching newscasts from all around the country, looking for potential stories for the show. This was a high-profile local case that became *really* high-profile, thanks to *48 Hours.*

The press rep said once they locate a story that might be interesting to their viewers, they contact the people involved, to see if they are willing to participate. Rita Brown remembered receiving a call from John Morgan, who was representing the family in the civil lawsuit against the Hills. He had already been contacted by the show. "He said *48 Hours* was probably going to call me, and they did."

As viewers across the nation sat riveted in their seats, watching the episode, many participated in an online chatroom about the episode debating Mary Hill's guilt or innocence. One of the strangest things was the choice of ads appearing during the show. Zoloft, a drug for depression, was heavily advertised. It featured a cartoon character who was so sad that viewers were probably depressed just watching it. Another ironic choice of ads was a promotion for the *Survivor* series. This one featured a woman, shackled to something, who called herself "She Devil," declaring, "She Devil still has some tricks left." One could only

The entrance to Wingfield North, a gated enclave of upscale homes located between Longwood and Lake Mary, Florida. *(Author photo)*

The Hill house sits at the end of a cul-de-sac. Surrounded by a wrought-iron fence and gate, it features a pool and cabana, putting green, and tennis courts. *(Author photo)*

Dennis Hill *(left)*, Rita Brown *(center)*, and Mary Hill *(right)* pose
in Brown's elegant tropical villa. *(Photo courtesy of Rita Brown)*

Jennifer *(left)* and Carrie Brown *(right)* sit on a four-wheeler.
(Photo courtesy of Rita Brown)

Zak Rockwell shows his expertise driving a four-wheeler.
(Photo courtesy of Keith Rockwell)

Rita and Carrie hug each other on Christmas morning.
(Photo courtesy of Rita Brown)

Big sister Jennifer hugs Carrie in front of a festive Christmas tree.
(Photo courtesy of Rita Brown)

Carrie and mom Rita pose on a ski trip.
(Photo courtesy of Rita Brown)

Carrie Brown's
yearbook photo.

Carrie celebrates her fourteenth birthday with her paternal
grandmother. It would be her last. *(Photo courtesy of Rita Brown)*

Greenwood Lakes Middle School in Lake Mary, where the three eighth graders had just attended the first day of school on August 7, 2000. *(Author photo)*

Dennis Hill drove his wife Mary and the three children, who were wearing seatbelts, in the back seat of his black 1996 BMW 740iL, to the Heathrow Exxon station. There, Mary Hill slid behind the wheel of the BMW and drove away with the three children in the back seat. *(Author photo)*

A sign before the curve close to the crash scene reduces the speed limit from forty-five to thirty-five miles per hour.

Mary Hill's wrecked BMW rests against the tree it impacted.

Emergency vehicles and workers quickly converged on the crash scene. The white van that Hill nearly collided with twice is parked in front of the Florida Highway Patrol (FHP) troop car.

FHP Corporal Phillip C. Wright's gut instincts and tenacity resulted in Hill's arrest for vehicular homicide and negligence.

The speedometer of Mary Hill's BMW shows it was traveling between seventy-three and seventy-four miles per hour upon impact.

The view of the car from the rear shows how it was twisted like a pretzel. Mary Hill, who was not wearing a seat belt, was thrown through the open window and survived the impact with minor injuries.

FHP Corporal Phillip C. Wright stands next to the back passenger compartment, which was crushed in approximately twenty-seven inches.

This photo of Carrie and Amy, more than any other, is the one people have come to remember. *(Photo courtesy of Rita Brown)*

The memorial tree where Carrie and Amy died on August 7, 2000. *(Author photo)*

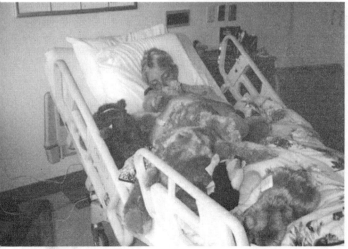

Zak Rockwell was in a coma for three and a half days after being freed from Mary Hill's BMW. *(Photo courtesy of Keith Rockwell)*

Hill's 2001 booking photo.

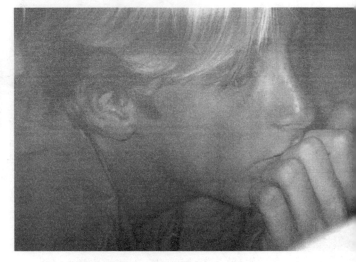

Zak Rockwell after awaking from the crash-induced coma.
(Photo courtesy of Keith Rockwell)

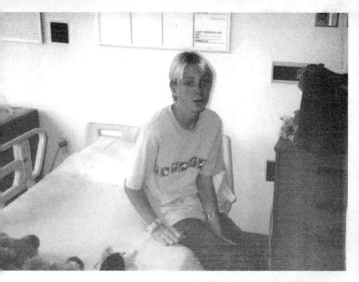

Zak sustained a closed-brain injury that left permanent damage.
(Photo courtesy of Keith Rockwell)

Zak and Keith Rockwell outside the now familiar Courtroom B at
the Seminole County Courthouse in Sanford. *(Author photo)*

Defense attorney Gerald Boyle claimed the cruise control cabling of the BMW was to blame for the accident.

Eighteenth Judicial Circuit State Attorney Norman "Norm" Wolfinger represents both Brevard and Seminole counties.

Lead prosecutor
Pat Whitaker.

Assistant SA
Bart Schneider.

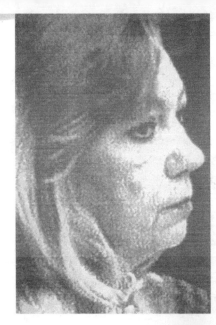
Mary Hill listens to her sentencing.

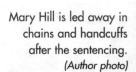
Mary Hill is led away in chains and handcuffs after the sentencing.
(Author photo)

wonder if she would manage to free herself in time to use some of those tricks.

Trial judge O.H. Eaton said the case received more media attention than any case he had ever presided over, in all his years on the bench. Yet, with all this coverage, all the interviews, all the investigating, no one ever discovered what actually happened in Mary Hill's BMW, from the time it left the intersection at Lake Mary Boulevard and Markham Woods Road and crashed into an oak tree.

Although former nanny Deane David's knowledge was secondhand, or speculation, as to what went on in Mary Hill's BMW during that fatal car ride, the two survivors of the ride had some recollections of the event. Zak Rockwell was able to remember some things early on, but some details were fading from memory as time went on. Mary Hill told what she recalled to Peter Van Sant, *48 Hours* interviewer, and later in her trial testimony. Her memory was very detailed, both times, down to conversations in her car. She may have hold David she didn't remember anything soon after the crash, but at some point in time, before the *48 Hours* interview, details of the incident apparently came back to her—vivid, detailed recollections.

Zak Rockwell, the only backseat passenger to survive, was able to relate some of his memories to FHP Corporal Phillip C. Wright about six weeks after the crash occurred. Keith Rockwell drove his son to the Lake Mary Police Department (LMPD) on Monday, September 18, 2000, for the interview. Also present with them were a court reporter, who worked for a local court-reporting service, ASA Jim Carter and Thomas

Neal, the attorney engaged by the Rockwells to pursue a civil suit against the Hills.

Veteran lawman Wright worked hard to put Zak at ease, while attempting to find out how much he remembered of the crash. The interview was short.

Corporal Wright was able to determine that Zak's memory of much of the event was sketchy. The last thing he really remembered with any clarity was the fifth period at school. His next memory was the crash—the first part of it, the skidding.

The next clear memory after that point was waking up in the hospital, four days after the crash.

"Do you remember how you got out of the crash?" Wright asked.

"I don't remember," said Zak, "but I was told that Mr. Hill pulled me out. My dad told me."

Wright asked Zak to think back to the first part that he remembered of the crash. "Do you remember this fairly well in your mind, or is it not so clear?"

"I remembered it when I started to wake up," Zak said, "and I didn't think anything about it. But then I look back on it, and I can see, like, my friends were sitting next to me, and Mrs. Hill was driving, so I can see what was going on."

"Okay," said Wright, "do you have an impression at this point of the . . . of any reason why the car would have been sliding?"

"She was driving fast and didn't think . . . and thought that her car could make it around the turn, but it didn't."

Wright asked, "But you don't remember her going into the curve?"

Zak didn't remember.

"But you do remember during the skidding of the car? Starting to rotate," he asked. When Zak said he did, Wright continued, "Do you have any memory of a feeling that was a car going at a fast rate, or was going at a normal rate, or it may have even been going slower than normal?"

"I had an impression," said Zak, "that it was going fast, because when I remember the car sliding, I remember seeing everything still going by."

"Okay. You say you remember things going by. How did that give you the opinion that perhaps the car was going fast?" asked Wright.

"Seeing the things going by would be at more than the speed of the speed limit. So it would be faster than a regular car would be going."

"So, in other words, and I don't want to put any words into your mouth," said Wright, "it seemed that the scenery outside was going by in a hurry?"

Wright patiently explained to Zak that he possibly knew how confused things were in his mind at the present, as Wright had once had a similar situation as a young boy in a bicycle accident. "I was about your age, and I ran into the back of a parked car. All I remember is looking up and seeing something big and black in front of me, and going over my handlebars.

"The next moment," Wright said, "I remember two altar boys carrying me off the altar at a church in Hendersonville, North Carolina. Then everything was really blotchy for the next year or so. It really bugged me, bad, that I couldn't remember the school year prior to it, or what happened after the car and I came into contact.

"And things [would] just kinda pop in here, and pop in there, with no particular order to them. Eventually everything kinda came back into place, and made me feel a lot better. So maybe that'll happen with you, too. But I don't think I would worry a whole lot about it.

"What I am gonna ask for your dad to do is if you get to this point, that you recall what transpired in the vehicle, from the time you got in it, until the time the crash happened, that we need to know about it very badly."

Both Carter and Wright cautioned him not to be influenced into thinking anything he might read or be told was actually a true memory. "You can't let people plant things in your mind," Wright said. "I've already had two or three people that have been referred to me as witnesses, that their only part is they drove by the scene and were stopped in the traffic caused by the crash. They had no contact with anybody prior to, at or after. So you're gonna be hearing a lot of things." Wright pointed to his head. "So it has to come from in here. Not from what people may tell you. I guess there's an old saying, believe nothing you hear, and only half of what you see. This'll be a good guideline to go by."

While she was in the hospital, immediately after it happened, Mary Hill may have told stepdaughter Heather and/or daughter Kaitlynn—as Deane David remembered—details of the crash. Those details may have been related to others as well; it's almost impossible to tell, as people's memories have faded in and out, as the case worked through the justice system over the period of forty-three months from the time of the crash until the trial began. It would be another five months after that, before the sentence was handed down—a few days shy of forty-eight months.

Perhaps letting her guard down during telephone conversations with her former employee may have actually brought memories back to Hill as she relaxed and chatted on the phone, although she would tell psychiatrists who interviewed her after the crash that she was having memory problems.

Deane David told civil suit attorneys John Morgan and Thomas Neal that she had related to Dennis Hill the conversation she had with Heather, regarding what Mary said happened, just four days before she participated in the deposition with them. "Mary doesn't remember anything about it," Dennis Hill told her.

"She doesn't remember anything." She assured the attorneys that was what Dennis Hill had told her. "And I didn't say, 'Is that selective memory?' Because, I mean, for a woman that [had] her ribs busted and her knee broken and her head's just fine— I mean, I could appreciate that to a point. I mean, I don't know about you, but I can speak for myself as far as being in a bad car accident. You do have a sense of loss of memory if there's a lot of tumbling or that going on, but the actual 'before it happened' is very clear in my mind, you know. You know what I'm saying?" David talked with Dennis Hill for almost an hour. "Trying to figure out how it happened. I mean, every day I'm sure he goes through it."

After David told him this, Dennis Hill told her they had "proved that it wasn't eighty miles an hour, that it was only forty-five. It was blown out of proportion," he contended.

David continued, "He still does not really know. I mean, he'll go through the rest of [his life not knowing]. Zak's the only one that can give us the answer of exactly what happened in that car. And I know that. I mean, we all have to know that."

David said Dennis had told her sometime around March, about the time Amy had called her to say her mother had been admitted to La Amistad, that things were getting bad and "that he didn't want to go anywhere."

His story to David about picking up the children from school was drastically different from the actual events as an accurate timeline of events developed as the case progressed: "That day, two hours before, he said he told Mary, 'I'll go pick the kids up from school.' And she says, 'No, I promised Amy that I'd go over there, you know, to pick her up on the first day of school. I'll do it.' She never picked those kids up after school, Amy and Carrie and Zak," David said.

When John Morgan asked her if Dennis had physically seen Mary or just talked to her on the phone, David was certain of what Hill had told her: "He physically saw her two hours before." She wasn't sure where that took place, but she was sure of what he told her: "He told me that he physically saw her."

David thought it was possible that Dennis Hill was having a car repaired: "I used to take him all the time, around the corner. As I was going home, I would drop him off to get the car picked up . . . right there at the Exxon. And I think that's what he was doing, [he] was getting his car. When he was only minutes behind Mary, that's how come he ended up at the scene of the accident.

"I don't know if she took him [to get the car]. I don't think she [did]. He said he saw her a couple of hours before that, so it could have been somebody at work that dropped him off to get his car."

Dennis Hill told David when he saw Mary a few hours before the crash, "'She was fine.' So he didn't feel like he had reason to worry for that one day in that one moment."

Mary Hill said she was worried about what was happening to the car after making the turn onto

Markham Woods Road, and she was very specific about those worries, according to her televised interview and her testimony during the trial. The last witness for the defense, Mary Hill told the court she remembered seeing Jimmy Arthur's van parked and then coming out of Heathrow as she drove by, maintaining she was already ahead of him before he even pulled out onto the roadway. She remembered stopping at the traffic light at the intersection, but did not recall having any difficulty with the car then, or having to back up from the center of the intersection.

She recalled the events after that: "I made a left-hand turn, but I made the wide turn. I stayed to the right. Even though I was making a left, I was close to the curbside.

"As I started to come out of the turn, like where the curb ends, I felt my rear passenger tire kind of slide a little. It was like . . . I explained it like I hit gravel, or I used to drive in Chicago and hit a patch of ice. It just like shimmied on me, and I wasn't in line with the front end.

"I let go of the accelerator and waited, thinking the car would right itself. [It] accelerated. It picked up speed. It started going faster. I applied the brakes . . . car kept going.

"I released the brake and applied it again. The car started going out of the lane. It was fishtailing.

"It happened very quickly. Everything was very quiet, and I just remember looking down at my dash, not at anything in particular. I didn't look at my odometer or anything, I just looked down at my dash. I said, 'Why won't you stop?'"

When Tim Berry, her attorney, asked, "To the car, you said, 'Why won't you stop?'"

"Yeah," she replied. The next thing she remembered

was waking up on the ground. She answered in the affirmative when asked if she had tried to brake the car and slow it, and negatively when asked if she ever intentionally accelerated and drove fast.

In the same testimony, she would later tell the court that she felt previous problems with the cruise control were "none that warranted saying anything about. I didn't perceive them as a problem. I thought there were times when I did use the cruise control that I would set it at fifty and it would jump a little bit more and I brought it down. I thought that was normal, but nothing major."

She would tell ASA Pat Whitaker that she immediately took her foot off the accelerator when she felt the right rear tire slipping: "The right rear seemed to go to the right, whereas the front end of the car was going straight." When she took her foot off the accelerator, "the car lunged. It started going much faster. The front end was, like, pulling it. I felt like the front end was way ahead of me. I can't explain it any other way," she told the court.

"It just started to really increase speed rapidly. I may not be using the right words, but that's the only way I can explain it."

She said she didn't initially apply the brakes when it happened, and when she did, she didn't floor the brake pedal because she was afraid of locking the brakes. The prosecutor asked her if she knew what an ABS braking system was and its purpose? She said she knew it was an antilocking braking system.

"So they will not lock?" asked Whitaker.

"So they say," she replied.

When asked about Jimmy Arthur's testimony, and whether or not she nearly sideswiped him, her reply was "Absolutely not."

"Are you saying it didn't happen?"

"No, sir, it did not."

Again Whitaker asked, "It did not happen?"

"No, sir," she said.

She repudiated his testimony as well about her speeding down Lake Mary Boulevard. "He says you were driving down that street at sixty-five to seventy-five miles per hour. You heard him say that," Whitaker asked.

"Yes, I heard him," Mary Hill answered.

Regardless of how the question was couched, she was unshakable in her reply that she was not speeding. She was emphatic that she did not shoot into the intersection as the traffic light turned red. After reiterating Arthur's testimony about that incident, Whitaker asked, "Are you saying now that did not happen?"

"No, sir," she said, "that did not happen. If I was that far out in the intersection, I would have made the turn."

Whitaker again described the witnesses who testified they saw just that happen, and their testimony "that you backed up your car so that you got your car out of the route of traffic."

"I don't remember that."

"Are you saying that did not happen?"

"I don't remember that," she repeated.

When asked about the witnesses' testimony that her "car engine was revving up there and even inching forward and taking off like a bullet shot when the light turns, are you saying that did not happen?"

"No, it did not happen."

"They said that you proceeded very fast through that turn," he persisted, "faster than anyone should be going through it. Are you saying that did not happen?"

"No, sir, it did not."

When he questioned her about her knowledge of the speed limit sign of forty-five miles per hour, and the warning sign of thirty-five miles per hour about the curve, and the blinking wildlife sign, she said she knew about them.

Before the trial, although it didn't air until afterward, on April 28, 2004, she told *48 Hours* correspondent Van Sant, "I just could not stop that car."

Jennifer Wilson, Mary Hill's daughter from her first marriage and the court-appointed guardian of Mary and Dennis Hill's surviving child, Kaitlynn, said, "I've heard both sides of the story—that they may have been arguing before they got to the service station, but I have no way of knowing if that ever happened. I just have not been able to talk to Mom about it. Not because I haven't had the opportunity, but Mom and I still have a very tenuous relationship at this point. What's the point? Anyone in her position, the sadness I feel for her, most of the time, is uncontrollable.

"I don't believe it about her erratic driving on Lake Mary Boulevard. There are other people who have come forward and said she wasn't driving erratically. So there's where the problem with my dad comes in. If he had just, regardless of the car's fault or not, had not been pushing toward suing BMW— even [if] it was, and I'm not saying that's it not, and just left it as a terrible accident. If he had left it as a terrible accident, and we don't know what went wrong, but regardless of the cause, it was a terrible accident. If he hadn't been pushing . . . I don't know."

CHAPTER 13

The mass of men lead lives of quiet desperation.
What is called resignation is confirmed desperation.
                              —Henry David Thoreau

Mary Hill was born September 27, 1950, in Chicago, Illinois, the Windy City, to a middle-class family. She lived in that area until she decided to move to Florida in the early 1980s. Her father, a truck driver, was killed in a traffic accident when a drunken driver crashed into his vehicle. She was fourteen years old, although she would sometimes tell people she was twelve or thirteen years old at that time. Regardless of her age, it had a tremendous impact on her, even to the point of causing her to deny the tenets of her Catholic upbringing and question why God had allowed such a thing to happen. Today, a child would receive grief counseling. The child would learn that anger and questioning a loved one's death are natural and a part of the progressive steps of grieving—she received no such counseling. She was left alone to question, to hurt and to sublimate her anger and rage at her loss.

Her mother, a housewife, never remarried. Mary

had one brother, who was two years older than she. When she was twenty-eight years old, he died from mesothelioma, asbestos poisoning.

According to documents entered as evidence in her trial, at the age of nine years old, she was sexually abused on at least three or four occasions by a family member. The documents reveal she said the man touched her genitals and forced her to touch his, although the abuse did not progress beyond that. She would later say she never had any nightmare or flashbacks about the episodes. Apparently, the reality of her life in the latter years of her second marriage were far more horrifying and mentally debilitating to her than the sexual attacks on her as a child, acts that must have been frightening and confusing to a child.

She remembered that her mother, a woman she described as being depressed her whole life, "was dying for thirty years." Her mother would discipline Mary once a month. She would spank her with a strap three times across the "butt." Later, when Dennis Hill cut off financial assistance to Mary after they separated, she credited her mother, who *actually* was dying, with helping her out financially, until her mom's death in September 2003. She also told a doctor that her mother was the only emotional support she was receiving during the troubling times after the car crash. "I am having a very difficult time and nothing seems to be going right for me," she told him.

Mary's daughter, Jennifer Wilson, had good memories of her grandmother. "My grandmother always lived by herself; she was a very independent, strong woman. She never wanted to relinquish her independence. They (Mary and Dennis) had tried to get her to live with them, from time to time, but there was so much chaos in the house, they just didn't need any more. [Also] I don't think she wanted to do that to herself.

"It would bother her if she couldn't vacuum every day, she was just one of those independent people. But my mom did finally convince her to move to Florida and they would get her a place in Florida. A house was too much, so they got her an apartment, then a little mobile home in a senior community nearby. After Amy died, she got really sick, and my mom, or someone at my mom's house, got her into a nursing facility. She had bone cancer, and she had been diagnosed with only six months to live, and it had spread to other parts of her body, and other complications. She had previously been at Deltona, but I wanted her close by. I took her to Mt. Dora, which is walking distance from my house, so we were able to visit her. Kaitlynn was already living with us at this point."

After graduating from high school, Mary worked in various jobs. She worked for six years as a plant manager in Illinois, then quit that job instead of accepting a job transfer to another section of the country. She then worked as a secretary, a career she would pursue until she became pregnant. At age twenty, Mary wed a Chicago cop, who was four years her senior. They had one child when Mary was twenty-four. They named their little girl Jennifer. After Jennifer's birth, Mary worked at a bank, opening new accounts. The union lasted eight years, until the husband proved unfaithful and the marriage ended.

After the divorce, Mary left the bank job and went to work for U.S. Research Company. In 1983, at age thirty-three, she married forty-three-year-old Dennis Hill, the owner of U.S. Research Company. She would soon find out this was no fairy-tale marriage, and her husband was not Prince Charming.

Mary has leveled charges against Dennis Hill that he denied to Peter Van Sant in a *48 Hours* interview. "God, no. How can you respond to something like that?" he stated.

What were the charges Hill so vehemently denied? Charges of sadomasochism, charges that he restrained her, slapped her . . . and more. In fact, family court would take the charges so seriously, a restraining order was issued against Dennis Hill for sexual violence and a threat of violence against Mary. The restraining order prevented him from contacting her or being in her immediate vicinity. The restraints extended also to their surviving daughter, Kaitlynn, who at the time was living with Mary in their still-beautiful home in Wingfield North.

After almost twenty-one years of marriage and many years together prior to that, in January 2003, the romance was finally over. It had been over for a long time. Mary Hill said she began experiencing mood disturbances, attributed to her marital problems, since she was in her mid-forties. She also experienced many physical problems as well. Mary Hill was living a life of financial privilege—a privilege sometimes withdrawn from her and her three daughters as a punishment when she angered Dennis Hill, usually over her discontent with his affair with her rival in Chicago. Finally, though, she told him she wanted him to move out. She told a psychiatrist that the thing that prompted her to ask for a divorce was that she found out Dennis Hill was going to give the ownership of their company to his mistress.

Although Dennis Hill denied Mary's accusations, she said Dennis became sexually gratified by sexual mutilation and pain—giving pain and receiving pain. She said he whipped her, resulting in bruises that left no scars, and twice in the last few years of their marriage, he forced himself on her. But it didn't end there. Dennis Hill, she said, compelled her to engage in group sex with another woman on at least one occasion. All the while, he had participated in numerous dalliances, maintaining a long-lasting affair with a married woman, with whom he had a child. During their marriage, she said, she had no extramarital partners. She denied his countercharges that she was a drug addict and an alcoholic.

By her own admission, she had legally taken Vicodin, off and on, since her twenties, for dental pain and headaches. She admitted to having a problem with it for six to eight months in 1999 and early 2000, needing something to get her through the day. Consuming as many as one hundred pills a week, she obtained them by circling the number on the doctor's prescription, to obtain more than he prescribed. Circling the number increased the amount prescribed, in doctor-pharmacist shorthand. She was also able to obtain Vicodin illegally from an Illinois supplier. Other than the Vicodin problem, she maintained to the psychiatrists who interviewed her at her defense team's behest that she had no other history of illicit or illegal substance abuse. Extensive sinus surgery in 1999, she felt, was responsible for her Vicodin addiction. She also told them she never took a drink until she was twenty, and thereafter would only take a drink occasionally. After she separated from Dennis Hill, she told them she did up her alcohol consumption to one wine cooler a night and a mixed drink once or twice a week.

The year 1999 seemed to have been an unusually distressful year for Mary Hill. It was at this time, she said, she became very angry and decided to confront her ongoing marital problems and saw a psychiatrist. She related that after an argument with her husband, she would begin again to take Vicodin secretly, after she had been detoxified and was off the drug. The Vicodin habit was not helping her depression. She still felt depressed and found herself crying a lot.

Her depression deepened and problems increased when on April 3, 2001, SCSO deputies came to her door in Wingfield North and arrested her. "I never thought I would be charged with a crime," she told *48 Hours.*

Dennis Hill told the same CBS reporter, "Life was good. Five minutes later, your life changes like you never thought it could change." Life did change, not just with the death of their daughter Amy, her friend Carrie and Zak's injury in the summer of 2000. The private lives of the Hills suddenly became very public, as both rumor and fact were passed around, each masquerading as the other. Finally it reached the point where it was difficult to distinguish one from the other. Mary Hill told one psychiatrist that the outcome of her trial had already been decided, played out in the media, before it ever came to court.

Neither Mary nor Dennis was talking to the press, except for cooperating with *48 Hours.* Other people who knew them and/or worked for them were not so reticent.

According to Pat Key, a former Nolan employee, "Dennis is very much a womanizer. When you look at him, you ask, 'Where is that at?' I think it's surely a thing with him that the money is the aphrodisiac, because he doesn't have a personality. Dennis is very dapper. He wears a hat, even though not many men do now, but Dennis wears one and looks very good in it.

"He is a very matter-of-fact businessman. He's personable, but he's not friendly, and he's the kind of guy who likes to flaunt what he has, but not in the same way Mary did, not as obvious.

"And that about Dennis being sexually deviant, like they talked about on *48 Hours,* oh yeah. Yeah, there's a story about Dennis and his prowess," which was known around the office.

Dennis Hill continued to deny allegations, but stories still cropped up, both from wife Mary and former employees.

By Mary Hill's own admission in court documents filed in the divorce, she claimed Dennis Hill forced her to participate in sex with another woman. She also claimed he was a sadomasochist, who liked to inflict pain on himself and others for sexual gratification. She aired this allegation very publicly, nationwide, in fact, on the *48 Hours* episode about the case. She revealed that he would beat her in a way that left no bruises.

"Mary and Dennis were swingers, that's the type of parties they would go to. Maybe they went to these parties because they didn't fit in at the country club, places where they lived, because these were people who looked up to them and they liked that," said Towne. "They were the people with the power and the money, they were the bosses.

"I don't think she would be the way she is, without him, and the unhappiness he gave her. I imagine that has to be hard to know your husband has another family that he spends a lot of time with . . . where the head office is. He was up there more often than he was down here—it wasn't like [saying, for example,] 'Oh, I got someone pregnant up in New Jersey'; it was, 'I have two families.'

"That made her very unhappy. When he wasn't in town, she was miserable and she would often cry. I wouldn't say she's a total monster; on the other hand, I would say he was. I guess he had the money."

Towne was a little more forgiving in his attitude toward Mary Hill than some other former employees were. "She was a difficult person to work for and be with, but she had her moments when she was nice. She wasn't always bad.

"I think it was a combination of things—the truly hideous relationship setup with Dennis, not having any friends, not being accepted in the community— she had nowhere to turn, no one to talk to about her problems. I think if she was a hard person, it was because she had to be.

"If I found myself in that situation, I wouldn't be able to leave the house and go to work. I'd just sit home and cry, but she had to harden herself, I think because she had to. If she was a mean person, it was probably a defense mechanism. I'm sure she was mostly unhappy, and I'm sure their relationship has had to do some damage to her self-esteem—sometimes it makes them feel better to pick on other people. That could be the reason she was [the way she was].

"I wish Dennis would have to take some responsibility for it. It's sad that he comes across looking like the caring, supporting husband, when you know he was getting ready to leave her anyway. He's been looking to bail out on her anyway. I don't think he'll stick around and support her once she's in prison.

Once the media stops looking at it, he'll bail. I'm sure he just doesn't want to look bad right now."

Faced with Mary's situation, Towne would have been a little more pragmatic in his treatment of Dennis Hill. "If it was me, I just would have divorced him and taken half his money. I don't know why she didn't. What a mess. I think it's just a shame. What people are not taking into account when they make her out to be such an awful person, her daughter just died. She lost someone, too. Especially knowing you did it, that you were driving recklessly, that's what killed your child, that's got to be hard to wake up to every morning. If she wasn't depressed before, that would certainly do it."

Towne's parting shot: "If she instigated the divorce, good for her if she did."

Jennifer Wilson knew what went on behind the closed doors of the Hill household. As a child, she had to deal with stepsiblings who hated her—a sentiment, she admits, she returned in kind, plus she had an increasingly unhappy mother. In addition to that, she had to deal with Dennis Hill's bizarre behavior toward her. It's one of the reasons she was desperate to remove her sister Kaitlynn from his custody. She knew what had happened to her as a child in Dennis Hill's home. When Dennis contacted Kaitlynn after the court had placed her in Jennifer's custody, he tried to bribe her to come spend time with him, according to Jennifer. "I told Kaitlynn," she said, "'Well that's just borderline prostitution and it will get to that level, Kaitlynn, don't get me wrong. He's done it to me as a child and is showing signs of doing it to you—don't go there.' Which is what my desperate act, and for other reasons, was to get her out of there." Jennifer had been strong-minded enough to resist his bribes and advances, but she was worried about what might happen to her little sister without her protection.

The divorce files reveal Mary Hill's allegations that Dennis Hill is a sadomasochist. One of the reasons the State of Florida gave custody of Kaitlynn to Jennifer Wilson was that Mary showed the child photos of her father's alleged sexual mutilation—the state declared them both unfit parents. Along with other incidents, Jennifer recalls that he would make sexual comments about Kaitlynn's body. "He did the same thing to me as a child," she said.

Jennifer's memories of her childhood in Dennis Hill's household were anything but pleasant. "He offered me money. He would be sitting on my bed when I woke up in the middle of the night. He would tell me to come into bed with him constantly—he would love me, he would be a lot nicer to me." Jennifer refused, so he would be mean to her afterwards in retribution. "But, he doesn't actually start until you start looking like a woman.

"He had gotten to the point of thinking he was indestructible, unobtainable, untouchable—his money would buy him out of anything." Jennifer recalled.

And then there was trying to deal with her mother's addictions and trying to convince Dennis to get help for her. "After Amy died, we tried everything. I would go over and say, 'Dad, this is a problem. Look at the woman.' She normally was a very thin woman—she was about five feet six inches and normally would weigh anywhere between one hundred fifteen to one twenty-five—she was very thin; that would be her very healthy, thin weight for her. I would go over there and she would weigh ninety-two pounds—and her face was swollen. I would go, 'She's doing drugs,' and no one would believe me. 'Oh no, she's not.' 'No, she's not.' 'No, she's not.' Give me a break. She's up all night and sleeps all day. 'Why won't you do anything?' He'd go, 'She's fine.'

"Well, if you knew someone had a drug problem or an alcohol problem, would you go get them a case of beer or a case of vodka? She couldn't drive. Somebody was supplying her with all that. Someone was filling her prescriptions—ninety Vicodin, ninety Percocets— somebody was taking her to the doctor to get them- refilled—and not standing up and saying, 'This is out of your control. This woman has a problem. We need to get her help.' Or, 'For self-preservation, get you and your kids out of there, if you are that kind of parent.'"

Jennifer recalled telling Dennis, "She is going to hurt somebody. You've got to help her. You've got to quit providing her with everything she needs. Quit giving her more drugs, quit finding more doctors that will write her prescriptions for her."

"She doesn't do drugs," Dennis would tell Jennifer. "You don't know what you are talking about. You don't understand anything, you just don't know what you are talking about. Just get out."

Even before the crash, Jennifer recognized the signs of drug use in her mother. She tried to get Dennis to get help for her mother. "Then it got ugly. You know, then I wasn't wanted around there." This was the time Deane David related when Mary moved Jennifer and her family from the pool house, after she went to Dennis about her mother's cocaine use. "It was just fight, fight, fight. Kaitlynn and Amy weren't allowed to talk to me on the phone. They couldn't e-mail me or they would get grounded. She, of course, didn't want me around, either. Because at this point, as an addict . . . and then Amy dies.

"I'm sure a big part of him blames himself, and I'm sure that's uncontrollable. I feel bad for that, because he used to see it, and he allowed the children to ride in a car. . . ."

Jennifer blames Dennis for her mother's mental condition. "That he aided her addictions, that he knew this was a very sick, troubled woman—a woman he drove to this state. You can only push someone so hard before they just give up."

CHAPTER 14

What anger worse or slower to abate than
lovers love when it turns to hate?
                                        —Euripides

Divorce can be an ugly business, and when there are
a lot of assets, it can get uglier, fast. When one party
is an aggressive, self-made millionaire, it can become
a no-holds-barred, free-for-all fight. The breakup of
a marriage is seldom civil, and Dennis Hill did tell a
national audience, "*The War of the Hills* is going be
more dramatic than *The War of the Roses*"—a movie that
Jennifer Wilson said, "He loved."

The notorious discontent of Mary and Dennis Hill
had already touched and tainted many lives before
they actually reached the point of separation in January 2003. All the different factions of their own
family were estranged from the parents—either Mary
or Dennis, or both—and from each other. The older
Hill siblings from Dennis's first marriage intensely
disliked Mary and her daughter Jennifer—although
they seemed to get along well with Amy and Kaitlynn. Jennifer, Mary's daughter from her first marriage,

was estranged from Dennis and was at odds, off and on, with her mother—although she got along well with Amy and Kaitlynn. Mary and Dennis were not getting along at all—although they got along generally with Amy and Kaitlynn. The only unifying people in the extended family were Amy and Kaitlynn. When Amy was killed in the car crash, it seemed to be the catalyst that caused the final destruction of the Hills as a family.

After Amy's death, Kaitlynn became the pawn of both her parents. As their former love hardened into hatred of each other and their desire to destroy each other grew, she became her parents' victim. She was the central person in her parents' struggle to cope with the tragedy, and in the breakup of their marriage. Dennis was calling Mary an alcoholic and a drug addict who was mentally abusive toward him and their child. Mary countered she was worried about the influence and effect of his "alternative lifestyle" on the girl. Eventually the state would step in and declare both parents unfit. She was first placed in foster care, just to get her out of the household, then in temporary care of her sister Jennifer, which the court later made permanent.

After Mary Hill kicked Dennis Hill out of the luxurious family home, things didn't get better, they got worse—much worse.

Jennifer Wilson described the last days her parents were living together: "With the support of no one around you, you feel solely alone, and then the way it came to end, they were fighting so badly. He left, and then Kaitlynn wouldn't go with him, she was afraid of him, or whatever. He came home, broke down a door and raped my mom. It was at this point she filed a report and got a restraining order against him." Court documents reveal Mary Hill claimed that after Amy's death, she twice had non-consensual sex with husband Dennis. "Then Kaitlynn became afraid of my mom because of the drinking."

As the marriage was dissolving, the Hills engaged attorneys outside the criminal trial attorneys to help each of them retain his share of the marital assets. It seemed that the battle would be long and drawn out, as neither party was cooperating with the other—and they were still yet a year away from the criminal trial.

As in the criminal trial, there were lots of attorneys involved and a change of judges. The criminal trial would have many defense attorneys and four judges before the trial began. The divorce/custody battle was a little more fortunate—it only had two judges. Chief Judge Bruce W. Jacobus, of the Eighteenth Judicial Circuit, reassigned the case in March 2003 to Judge Donna L. McIntosh after Judge James E. C. Perry recused himself from further participation in the case.

Mary Hill wanted to stay in the Wingfield North home. She also wanted Dennis Hill to pay the payments on the house and the attendant upkeep and maintenance fees. She asked that he pay her support, give her exclusive use of the new red Mercedes convertible, while he made the payments and paid insurance on it, plus provide health insurance for her. She also requested the court to make him pay her attorney's fees. After all, hadn't she worked in his company for twelve years, helping to build up all the assets? She was no longer able to work, but he still ran the operation, and the business had been very successful. Also at question was: what happened to some of the properties, such as the beach condominium and One Business Place investments? She wanted a history of their sale, as well as appraisals on other properties.

Oh yes, she wanted him thrown in jail for thirty days until he complied with all the demands. (He didn't go to jail.) All of this happened in February 2003.

Dennis filed a counterpetition for dissolution, asking in a long list of items to have the primary exclusive use of the marital home and sole custody of Kaitlynn. He also wanted Mary to stop making statements to Kaitlynn that he felt would damage their father-daughter relationship, as well as to stop abusing him physically. His plan was to ask the court to appoint a master to conduct a private sale of the Wingfield North home, dividing the profit between the two Hills, after the expenses of the property were paid.

Both parents wanted custody of Kaitlynn. Dennis charged that Mary was "physically and emotionally abusive" to both him and Kaitlynn, and that she was "addicted to various substances, including alcohol." His attorney supported those allegations with a Petition for Dependency, filed by the Department of Children & Family Services, dated April 10, 2003. Dennis asked protection from Mary for himself and for the benefit of Kaitlynn. The injunctive relief motion filed stated that he believed "both himself and the minor child are in danger because of the conduct" of Mary. The motion contained a litany of charges against Mary, including throwing Kaitlynn out of the house at the end of March, and alleged the child had been locked out several other times. She was unable to go to her father's nearby home when this happened because of the restraining order against him. Mary also had once left her at dance class, not picking her up in the evening when it was over.

It went on to state that "Kaitlynn was afraid to ride in a car driven by her mother, due to her erratic driving, or to go home because of the threats that have

been made against her. Kaitlynn has great fear of her
mother. Her mother has mood swings, and has threatened to kill them both by driving into a tree. She
drives erratically, speeding and swerving in and out of
traffic." It also charged Mary with chronic alcoholism
and of driving under the influence of drugs and
alcohol.

It accused her of placing "the child at imminent
high risk of further physical and emotional abuse and
neglect." Dennis did not want Mary to know the "location of any residence where their child, Kaitlynn,
would reside" with him, citing he feared "that ir-
reparable harm and damage would be caused to
himself and the minor child, Kaitlynn, in the event
an injunction is not issued against the wife."

Back and forth, motions and requests were filed on
behalf of both parties, as Mary and her attorneys
wanted to have access to financial records, to determine what remained of the marital assets and how
much had been obtained for those sold. They maintained Dennis had "systematically removed the Wife
from title and ownership of a majority of the assets and
placed them with known and unknown parties," saying
he "utilized paramours and business partners to assist
in his financial dealings." Dennis and his attorneys
would counter that they couldn't give that information,
as Mary was in possession of all the documents in
their marital home from which he was "ousted." While
they were fighting over custody of Kaitlynn, Mary requested the court require Dennis Hill to "submit to
a full psychological evaluation to determine his fitness
to exercise shared parental responsibility of the minor
child," should the Department of Children & Family
Services "relinquish jurisdiction."

In April, Dennis Hill's attorney, joined by Mary's

attorney, tried to block public access, including for the press, to the court hearings in regard to the divorce and custody case. They wanted to have the court files sealed, on the basis that if the information were publicized, it would cause harm to Kaitlynn. The request stated, "There is no essential need or right that requires the exposure of Kaitlynn Hill to an invasion of her privacy which may subject her to ridicule, humiliation and embarrassment."

During that hearing, Norma Ragsdale, the guardian ad litem protecting Kaitlynn's interest in the court proceedings, agreed the hearings should be closed. She described Kaitlynn as "a peacemaker-type person. She wants to keep everything smooth and calm around her." Ragsdale told the court that Kaitlynn "loves both her parents and she seems very torn by the situation that she is in."

That motion failed, but Dennis Hill still had a lot of tricks up his sleeve.

Shortly after Dennis asked for injunctive relief, Maryellen Humes, investigator for child-protective services with SCSO, an authorized representative of the Florida Department of Children & Families, asked the court to declare Kaitlynn dependent, taking away custody of both parents and placing her with a third party. A guardian ad litem was acting on her behalf while she was placed in the temporary legal custody of Jennifer and Michael Wilson.

Humes cited some of the same incidents in Dennis's previous motion—such as Kaitlynn's being locked out of her house, the erratic driving of her mother and fearing going home because of threats made against her—in her report to the court. She also included information that Mary Hill had told Kaitlynn: Dennis had sexually abused her older sister

Jennifer, a charge both Jennifer and Dennis have denied.

Mary's mental-health problems also were revealed, including the fact that she suffered "from a chronic major depressive disorder . . . for which she has been in therapy, had shock treatment and is under medication." Her multiple addictions were cited, as well as the episodes where she exhibited suicidal tendencies, threatening to kill herself and Kaitlynn, and wishing Kaitlynn had died in the car crash instead of Amy. "She has, therefore, placed the child at imminent high risk of further physical and emotional abuse and neglect," Humes reported to the court.

In addition: "The mother has attempted to show the child, Kaitlynn, pornographic material depicting what is believed to be her father, Dennis. The mother has been unable to separate her anger towards Kaitlynn's father and continues to berate Kaitlynn with accusations of mistreatment towards the mother by the father." In part, because of Mary's inability to control her anger in Dennis's regard, and taking it out on Kaitlynn, Humes theorized that Mary "is unable to meet the safety, well being, emotional and psychological needs of the minor child."

Humes informed the court that "there had been several reports on the hotline regarding the emotional state of the family." She reiterated a claim of Mary's that she wasn't in any kind of mental treatment "because no one would treat her because of her pending criminal trial and the notoriety the family is living under. This is not true according to her therapists," Humes reported. "On information and belief, her therapists ended her therapy as there was no one there qualified to treat her after her original psychiatrist, therapist and/or addiction specialist left the practice."

Humes came back to the subject of mental abuse. "The mother has subjected the child to mental abuse in other ways as well. She has accused Kaitlynn's father of sleeping with her grown daughter, Jennifer. This has been emphatically denied by both Jennifer and Dennis Hill.

"Kaitlynn had a cat," she continued, "that had been mauled by a dog the father had purchased. The mother made no attempt to get the cat to the vet, she left it to die, stating it was Kaitlynn's father's fault for buying the dog and he would have to take care of it." She wasn't finished. She described how Mary had "virtually become a recluse in her own home. She did not leave her bedroom for most of the past two and a half years. There has been no collateral contact to say she has participated in any part of Kaitlynn's life. Mr. Hill was responsible for taking her to and from any activity she had to participate in. Kaitlynn reports having minimal contact with her mother, and when she does, all her mother does is blame everyone for her depression and all the problems she has."

It seemed things were not going well in this regard for Mary, but Dennis jumped right on the fact that Humes did not hold him responsible for any of the mistreatment of Kaitlynn.

His attorney filed a motion within five days, requesting custody be given to Dennis, stating that Dennis was prepared to accept her into a home he had waiting for her. In the end, that motion was not granted. Jennifer was granted permanent custody of her sister Kaitlynn.

Dennis Hill was just getting into his pace, though. The line "Payback is a bitch" was obviously a page out of Dennis Hill's *How to Manage a Divorce* manual. Sometime in August of the same year, he canceled Mary's health insurance. She found out about the cancellation during a five-day stay in the hospital for tests. She was discharged for lack of insurance.

She then found out he had canceled her automobile insurance, when she received a letter to that effect from Tallahassee. Things were definitely getting worse. He was three months behind on payments for the red Mercedes convertible she was driving.

Could things get any worse? Most definitely, yes. While she was trying to cope with the latest of Dennis's tricks, the water to the house was shut off. She didn't have any water for four days, except what she could dip out of the swimming pool. She boiled it to use as bathwater and gave it to her dog to drink. It's probably a very good thing that she did boil it, as the pool had to be shut off, and the water from the well outside was contaminated. She didn't have the $15,000 to repair the problem.

By October, Dennis Hill was pulling a few more cards out of his bag of tricks. He had failed to meet the support payment due on the first of the month, and judging by the calls Mary was getting from creditors, he wasn't paying the bills, either. The bank was calling about the mortgage, as well as a second mortgage holder and the homeowners association dues were past due. She didn't have to worry about creditors' phone calls for long, though. Dennis had the phone service disconnected at the house and she didn't have the money to pay the outstanding bill or a deposit for reactivation.

At one time, there were four different phone lines in the home, but when Kaitlynn was removed from the home in April, Dennis called the phone company and had Kaitlynn's phone line disconnected, along with two others, leaving just Mary's phone line in service. At the same time, he also had the phone company transfer the outstanding bill into Mary's name. First there were four; then there was one; then there were none. Dennis Hill was turning into a pretty good magician.

By chance, she found out that he had listed their home for sale without her permission and against a court order. He also had listed the house where he was now living in Heathrow—this was also a marital asset. She told the court she feared he was liquidating all the assets, preparing to move out of state. Her plea was make him stop or find him in contempt of court.

Dennis, however, was not only withholding support from Mary, he was ignoring his court-ordered obligation in paying Kaitlynn's support as well. He was directed to pay support to Jennifer and Michael Wilson for Kaitlynn, beginning in April 2003. They had to petition the court in September of that year to enforce the directive. He still refused to pay and had not paid any of it as of January 2005, telling the Wilsons he was unemployed and was going to have to go on unemployment.

Last seen, the dissolution and custody file filled three huge folders in the Seminole County Clerk of Courts Office. As more petitions are filed, and allegations leveled, it is sure to grow. In fact, it is growing as Dennis Hill petitions the court to force Jennifer and Michael Wilson to give him more access to Kaitlynn, saying they are denying him visits, contact and the ability to see her when they changed her therapist to one near where they live. They are having difficulty struggling with the fees associated with answering his motions. The Wilsons were warned he would likely play the "lawyer game" with them, trying to bleed them financially.

Last heard from, the Wilsons were to appear with Dennis Hill in family court in mid-January 2005, on the issue of the unpaid support payments. "There was no hearing," said Jennifer Wilson, "he skipped town." The support remained unpaid. Magician Dennis Hill finally made himself disappear. The question is, when will he reappear? And when he does reappear, will he be required by the court to pay the back support?

Perhaps he had just been working up to this finale for his act. He certainly made the mansion in Wingfield North disappear. While Mary was still living in it, it was falling into a state of disrepair, which progressively became worse. Dennis stopped making payments on it and the bank foreclosed.

CHAPTER 15

Many who seem to be struggling with adversity
are happy; many amid great affluence,
are utterly miserable.

—Tacitus

Jennifer Wilson has said she and her husband,
Michael, and their two sons have made Kaitlynn a part
of their immediate family. There have been a lot of
compromises and they have found creative ways of
coping with adding a teenager into the young family,
but they wouldn't have it any other way.

They have found that they are tested almost daily,
coping with answering and filing expensive motions
and appeals in regard to their custody of her. They
have worked on trying to make ends meet, with the
added burden of Dennis Hill not paying the child support payments he was supposed to pay. But they have
prepared to fully safeguard Kaitlynn from what they
have perceived as real harm, if she ever left their
home.

The transition into a tightly knit family was terribly
strained when Kaitlynn first came to live with them,

just from travel logistics. Jennifer recalled she was driving all the time—all the way from their Lake County home, every school day, to keep Kaitlynn in school classes there, plus to dance classes also in Seminole County. It was crazy. But they were trying to do what would be best for Kaitlynn. Life seems to be working out better for them now, since they have been able to move everything closer to their home.

"Kaitlynn was very much interested in dance before (when she lived with their parents), but the thing about dance was, she would go to dance six days a week—she would go Monday through Saturday—she would be at dance. She would leave school (she would ride the bus home) or would be picked up from school. She would be taken to dance and leave dance between nine-thirty and ten P.M. and grab something to eat. Then she would go home, do a little bit of her homework, or whatever, and go to bed and then start the whole day over again. And then on Sunday, she either had a free day at piano or something else. Dennis was very much into teaching classes there (the music school), he had business relations there with the teacher.

"It got to the point where Kaitlynn told me, it wasn't her thing anymore, she loved it, but didn't know she was supposed to do anything different. She was so controlled.

"When Kaitlynn came to stay at our house, she couldn't tell you if she liked vanilla or chocolate ice cream. 'I don't know.' Do you like strawberry because you have red hair? 'Okay, I'll have strawberry.' She was totally controlled, one hundred percent. She had just lived in her room, and lived being taken around place to place.

"I continued to drive her constantly, but it was very

far for me to drive, so I did cut it (dance classes) back
to three days a week. I couldn't drive it. . . . I mean,
I had no life—I have two kids and a husband. I believe
in doing things for your kids, but I don't believe in
giving up your life entirely for your kids. I think you
make giant concessions for them, but I need at least
one night a week to myself. You know, I'll give you
three or four, as you need, but you're going to have
[to] give for me, so there is still some small piece of
me left. That might not be everyone's opinion, but
that's mine.

"It was an hour or more drive there, depending on
traffic. I had to wait there—otherwise you had to
drive all the way back—and I was already driving her
to school every morning, so she could continue out
her school year at the old school. I was driving the
whole time. It was insane. But she didn't want to go
[to dance class].

"We moved her school, then moved her court-
appointed therapist, not the one Dennis had chosen.
That one (Dr. Mara) was very close to his work—it was
an hour and thirty minutes one way (travel time)—
and the therapist didn't have after-school hours. She
(Kaitlynn) was missing a whole day of school a week
because of it.

"That's what we were just in court about. I had just
changed [the] therapist to a nearby one, and Kaitlynn
wasn't wanting to go anymore [to Dr. Mara], because
Dennis was dominating all the sessions. I changed
[therapists] basically because Kaitlynn almost failed the
eighth grade, because she would miss a day a week of
school. Going there took pretty much the whole day.
She was really beginning to fail from missing school.
So, I just needed something that was more close by. I

was missing work and she was missing school and we were both struggling. So I changed her.

"I didn't do that through the courts, ignorantly. I didn't realize I had to. I just thought the important thing was for her to be in therapy. So he (Dennis) is taking us back to court. This is the man who hasn't paid a dollar of child support, none, since she was released into my custody. Oh, of course he's supposed to. We have to go back to court again; he's almost at the twenty-thousand-dollar mark at this point.

"This is the man who says we don't allow him to talk to or see Kaitlynn because we took her out of therapy. Well, he never e-mails her. Actually, he did e-mail her a joke once. It was a picture of Macaulay Culkin, the little *Home Alone* boy. He had his hands up to his face, going, 'Oh no.' Then there's a picture of Michael Jackson. She didn't get the joke and there was a link to go to, so she thought that explained the joke. It was a hard-core porn Web site. But that's not all. When she wanted to load a little game program on her computer, she couldn't get it on there. I thought there must be enough space for it, it wasn't that big a program. When I looked to see what the problem was, I found he had downloaded all kinds of porn pictures onto her computer.

"He never writes her. He never calls her and says 'let's go to lunch'—he used to, until my mom's sentencing, when he attacked me in the courtroom and threatened my life, that was when he stopped talking. And Kaitlynn stopped completely, too. His attempts of contact before then were 'If you come stay with me, I'll give you a hundred dollars.' 'If you come spend the night with me, we'll get you a phone.' Blatant bribery.

"Mike, my husband, is a horse trainer, that's what we do for a living. We own our own business. We personally own four horses, if you include Kaitlynn's horse, Burning Love. She calls him Baby Love—he's her project. But mostly, we train high-end animals, high-end Arabians. I don't do any boarding of any kind. We don't do any schooling of people, just horses.

"We go to the nationals every year. We go on the show circuit, that's our job. I'm breeding manager here at the farm, that's my job. Mares come in from all over the world to be bred, plus we ship out all across the United States. It's not like a boarding stable."

While the Wilsons have struggled with their daily lives, as well as trying to satisfy court orders, they have worked their way through the trauma that has torn their family apart. Jennifer has counseled her younger sister to try to reach a place within herself, where she can have a relationship with her father.

"I regret not having a relationship with my dad and have told Kaitlynn on several occasions, 'You will regret not having a relationship with your dad, and unfortunately, it seems like you are going to have to be the strong one, the parent, the respectable one, or whatever you want to call it, in the relationship. But you are going to have to find a way to even it out for yourself, so you can handle it on your own terms. If you don't have one completely, you will regret it. I know this from experience, no matter how tainted it is. At least be on a Merry Christmas basis.'

"He didn't send her a card, or a Christmas present, nothing. He's claiming unemployment and he can't pay child support, because he's going to be filing for unemployment. Okay, so you have two Mercedes, two SUVs, you have two Infinities, plus the house in Heathrow, which was totally remodeled, all new furniture, plus all the furniture from my mom's house, two grand pianos, all of her very expensive items. . . . You know if he needs to make some money, let's have a yard sale."

Her answer to his plight: "You know you're driving around in your Mercedes, and yes, it's two years old. So is my Honda. I loved my little GTP Grand Prix, but when Kaitlynn moved in to stay with us, we had huge financial things we needed to rearrange, because my dad hasn't given us a dime. And I had to sell it. And I got a little Honda Accord, two-door, and it's a '99 and I love it, it's a great car. Kaitlynn can drive it, and I don't feel it's too much of a car, like the GP would have been for her. We made sacrifices.

"How can you say you want your child to come stay with you, but you are going to be on unemployment and can't pay a dollar's worth of child support? In all the years she has been with us, never has he asked, 'Are you okay? How are you holding up through this?' Nothing. When Amy died, nobody went there for her. It was like, 'Kaitlynn how are you?' 'She's fine; she's strong; she's going to be fine through all this.' She never cried. The only time I saw her cry was at the wake.

"I have never known anybody who died, neither of us did. Amy was the first. So I wouldn't go see my sister in the coffin. I refused. My dad made Kaitlynn go before everybody was at the wake. He made her go in there and see her. She came out screaming and just grabbed me, and was going on and on and on, and I couldn't understand her, what she was saying. I was like 'Calm down, what's wrong?' 'It's not her, it's not her.' 'What are you talking about, it's not her?' She just freaked. I guess she (Amy) had just been hurt so much and in so many places, and bones broken in her face, that it didn't look like Amy. That is the only time

Kaitlynn will tell you she cried, and that's weird, because they were very close."

Jennifer worried that Kaitlynn hadn't been able to cry, but she has taken comfort in knowing that Zak is still there for her, out of all the group of friends from the old neighborhood. "Carrie was very much a friend of Kaitlynn's, just as she was to Amy and Zak. To this day, every time we've been there (in court), she and Zak will sit down and talk and goof around about old times, and goof around about new times. It's hard, personally, because it's his family against our family; it's our sister—and our mom that's up there, but they don't forget what they had. They are really close. All those guys were inseparable, it was like a little clan. The little group of them (Amy, Kaitlynn, Carrie, Zak, the Hartzell girls—Alexis and Jessica), they really were inseparable.

"I don't know that much about the Hartzell girls now. I do know that their mother did sign off on their adulthood before they hit adulthood, emancipated them . . . either one or both of them. I knew Jessica, I never knew Alexis very well.

"On top of Zak doing well, Kaitlynn is doing well." She remembered the turning point, when Kaitlynn couldn't bear her home life anymore. "Kaitlynn called me from the dance studio. 'Please come get me, I don't want to go home.'

"First of all, she had gotten into a big fight with Mom at home. I told her to go to the office when she got to school and call HRS. They took her home and talked to my mom for a while, and, of course, my mom got really, really mad and she, of course, was fighting with my dad, and he was using it as a pawn in the divorce at this point. Otherwise, why would he leave Kaitlynn in that environment? Then she took her to the dance studio and there was the terrible [driving] incident there—that's when she called me and said, 'Come get me.'

"She was put into a foster home, because Dennis wanted it," Jennifer elaborated. "He has told Kaitlynn to this point, 'I would rather you be in a foster home' than with [Jennifer]. 'If you don't want to be with [me], then you can go into a foster home.' And that has been his stance.

"In the first foster home, there were ten other kids. Come on. She freaked. Kaitlynn hit bottom there. She was only there for, like, four days; then I finally got them to release her to me. My house hadn't finished being built yet, so we rented a hotel room at the Marriott in Lake Mary.

"A guy I had worked for, a really nice, rich man, he told me, 'You know what? That little girl deserves a night out. You guys can go stay at a hotel for the next couple of days at the Marriott, in Lake Mary. Order all the room service you want, all the movies you want, and kick back.' So we did. We went to that new Marriott that had just been built, while my house was being built.

"We were just staying in a one-room studio until the house was finished. My kids were in Canada, because our lease on our apartment was up, and the builder had said our house would be done. It wasn't. Then they said two weeks—the inevitable two weeks. We rented the studio, the kids were in Canada, and two weeks turned into thirty days, and we felt like killing ourselves—we hadn't seen the kids in a month. Here we were in this crappy little two-hundred-square-foot room, and we had to get out. Anyway, the house was finished and we all moved in, and luckily, we had just bought a four-bedroom house. We had a bedroom for Kaitlynn, so she moved in.

"We moved into one of those neighborhoods, where it's kind of cookie-cutter, but everybody knows everybody and all of her best friends are within walking distance. I have been kind of extremely hard on her, because she did go from being controlled completely, then what happens to a teenager when you take away control? It's wow! We wheeled that back in fast. You know it got hard for the first little bit, because I'm her sister and, you know, 'It's why would I listen to you?' I had the times when I'm goofing around with her like I'm her sister; then I have to decide, we can't go down that road.

"I'm surprised how she refuses to want to go back [to Dennis], even in those times when your sister is coming down on you, or your brother is coming down on you. (You don't refer to Mike as a brother-in-law or Jennifer as a half sister, or you will absolutely insult Kaitlynn.) Her brother and sister are coming down on her and she has to listen to them, you know. Maybe we did things that didn't agree with her; I don't know, I've never had a teenager to raise.

"I've told her, 'I am going to force you to make decisions. I will not tell you what to do or make your decisions for you. I am going to let you make bad decisions, and let you live out the consequences of those bad decisions.' For instance, she thought she would go on a joyride with my car, and that's before I got rid of that car (the Grand Prix). It was just a very powerful car, a little sports car, and first of all, she was fourteen years old. She wasn't going anywhere, but, you know, you don't go take out your dad's Mustang Cobra for a little joyride.

"She got grounded really bad, and for a very long

time. And she stuck to it, and never griped, and I expected her to be like other kids: 'Well, screw this, I want to go back and live with Dad,' but never once did she say that. She's, well, 'like I need that.'

"Her grades aren't the best, but they are A's, B's and C's, not D's. I would like to see more A's and B's, but she's working hard and she's taking pride [in her schoolwork].

"I don't push her toward the horses, but I gave her a project, the baby, and she has taken huge interest in it. Here I have been working my ass off my whole life, and this girl has, like, God-given talent of riding, and it irks me to death. It must be the balance, all that dancing. I bust my ass and she jumps on the same horse, and it's ta-dah, and, like, I go, I spent years of work and she's, like [riding by] osmosis.

"I don't know if that's her niche, or if it's just me and because it's available, but horses are fun for girls. She has been going to shows, and because she has me and Mike, and has higher-end animals, she is undefeated at this point. But I told her, 'You only have a few more years of seventeen-and-under before you are having to go into tall competition,' because she will be judged on her quality of animals, as well as herself. She does have me with a backup of quality animals, but that's only a very small part of it, most of it is her. She is unanimously undefeated at this point. I don't interfere, she picks which classes she wants to do; she's coming along very well."

Jennifer was asked to verify Deane David's testimony in regard to Kaitlynn. This was a deposition where David told state prosecutor Pat Whitaker that Kaitlynn had told her what happened in regard to the actual car crash.

Whitaker had asked David, "She didn't say anything

you recall about being upset with Amy in the car or any other people in the car?"

David's answer was "No . . . because that was my theory, because the kids are in the backseat of the car and she just kept saying, she doesn't remember, she doesn't remember, she said. . . . Wait, I have a comeback here. Kaitlynn told me at the beginning of the accident that she said that her mother told her in the hospital that all she did was turn back and say something to Amy, and she didn't remember anything after that. That's what Kaitlynn told me that Mary told Kaitlynn. That's all she did was turn back to look, you know. And I'm thinking the only reason you would do that is if you are angry and instead of looking through the rearview mirror when you're mad, because she's very impulsive with her temper, I can see her jerking back, or swinging or whatever."

Jennifer didn't mince words. "I don't think Kaitlynn said that to her. It was days before she (Mary) was able to talk. Even if she was able to talk, it was nonsense. Like when I saw her the first time, it was like 'my clothes they cut,' she was just gone. She wasn't making any sense. The other thing is, Kaitlynn won't talk to my mom about it.

"She (David) didn't even work for them at the time. She was actually asked to leave the house when she came over after the wake was held."

But there were more important things on Jennifer's mind as she juggled her work, caring for her family and dealing with the aftermath of Dennis and Mary Hill's breakup. There were still so many unanswered questions.

"They owned the old Anheuser-Busch estate on the west coast, along with Treasure Island properties, three New Smyrna Beach condos—two rentals and one they kept for their personal use. Dennis disposed of all those after the crash. He also owns lots of property around Florida and in Illinois, especially southern Illinois. He's not destitute like he's claiming. He owns double digits of cars. My mom is trying to find out in the divorce what's sold and where things are. She didn't sign anything, so she thinks her name must have been forged."

But Jennifer is long accustomed to dealing with Dennis Hill and his fickle temperament. "There was a time when I was in college, because she (Mary) found out the baby had been born and she was angry. Her power was shut off, all her credit cards were canceled, I was told that I was no longer to be in school, my car was reported stolen, all within twenty-four hours. He stopped being mad and then everything was turned back on.

In a dramatic phone call to Jennifer, Mary phoned her and frightened her so badly, Jennifer immediately flew home. "I was at Southern Illinois Carbondale and flew to St. Louis, then to Florida, and found her with pneumonia, catatonic on the floor. He was too busy to make it down there for a little bit, so I had to stay with her. The girls were with her, but they were very young, so I was down there for a couple of weeks, and, of course, had failed all my classes by that point. I was unable to return to school, because he would not pay for someone who would fail out of college.

"Until Amy died, he mostly stayed in Illinois. He was rarely down here. After Amy died, he started staying more, for apparent reasons. My mom pretty much couldn't deal with it anymore, and then it got even worse." Jennifer didn't feel Dennis's presence was beneficial. "The more he stayed, the worse it got.

He would never bring the family together, he kept us all at odds. He would fan the flame, so to speak.

"I thought, too if that defense had not been used, the outcome would have been different. We tried to tell Mom that, but Dennis would say, 'This is what I need to sue BMW.' Now he doesn't have to go through with a terrible divorce that had been filed. Now he doesn't have to deal with this woman who obviously has many mental issues, as well as addictional issues. He doesn't have to go through all his assets, or splitting up any of his assets. She goes to jail; it goes away.

"He threw all my mother's clothes away when he went back to the house. She has nothing. He got rid of the dogs, not even a week after she was sentenced. Before my mother was sentenced and after the verdict was given, he went directly over to her home that day and moved in that very day. He moved in, started rearranging and disposing of things that very day. Her dog was an Akita; he took the other dog, a husky, to the pound and had it destroyed. Her lawyer's son took the Akita, because she didn't want it destroyed as well. It was the dog she considered her dog.

"He's now on his fourth or fifth divorce lawyer. Every time they get to a motion to get things going, he gets a new lawyer and they have to start all over again."

And that's exactly what Jennifer, Michael and their two young sons, along with Kaitlynn, have done as well. They have started all over again, trying to do the best they can within the situation they find themselves.

CHAPTER 16

Women are catching up as aggressive drivers
though they're less overt. They are more seethers.
—Dr. Leon James, aka Dr. Driving

The case the prosecution would have to prove against
Mary Hill was whether or not she drove in such a
reckless manner that someone was bound to be hurt
or killed. Jim Carter, the felony intake supervisor in the
state attorney's office when Corporal Wright brought
the case to them in fall 2000, hired Hans Fuehrer, an
accident reconstructionist, to give him a second opinion on the FHP conclusions about the crash.

Hans Fuehrer agreed with the FHP that Hill was traveling through the curve at approximately seventy-
three miles per hour, nearly forty miles above the
recommended speed. Sergeant Ritter, of the FHP,
would recall that Fuehrer agreed with their investigation report and the conclusions reached by FHP. He
thought they were a little lenient in their treatment of
the driver of the crash vehicle.

Practically everyone who drives has encountered at
some time a driver who seems to be driving far too fast,

who may be weaving in and out of traffic. Sometimes this motorist is even passing vehicles on the wrong side, or blowing his horn at other drivers, gesturing at people or swearing at them. Is that common, usual behavior? An expert on reckless driving, speeding and road rage, Dr. Leon James, a psychology professor at the University of Hawaii, says it is a behavior that is on the increase nationally.

On his Web site, www.drdriving.org, some of Dr. James's statistics leave the mind reeling. He says road accidents are responsible for approximately 1.5 million deaths annually. In the United States, approximately proximately 42,000 people are killed as the result of traffic accidents, with approximately 6.5 million injuries resulting from traffic accidents. The monetary toll is high as well. He estimates the annual cost in the United States is $200 billion.

He maintains that the majority of "driver error" is due to "lack of emotional intelligence behind the wheel." He says drivers can change this attitude themselves.

He revealed some startling information garnered from his study. "Drivers are stressed out, threaten each other, are in a bad mood, terrorize their passengers, and often fantasize violent acts against each other," he says.

The rage that some drivers display behind the steering wheel may actually have nothing to do with what is going on in traffic. They may actually be mad at someone at work or in a personal relationship. They may have had a bad experience at the mall or found their fast food order was wrong after they drove away. Whatever the reason, they are expressing that anger once they get behind the steering wheel of their car—a place where they are all powerful, and anyone can become their victim.

Dr. Kirshna Gujavarty, a Long Island psychiatrist, suggests, "It's not always a good idea to get into the car after you've had a fight with your mate. That's when you tend to drive faster and more aggressively and that's how the trouble starts."

"Women are catching up as aggressive drivers though, they're less overt. They are more seethers," said Dr. James.

Dr. James attributes the trend towards more people engaging in aggressive driving as a result of having less control in their lives. When they get into their car, something that does respond to their wishes, they become invincible. "In automobiles, we have an increased (but false) sense of invincibility," he explains. Other drivers no longer exist as human beings, they are "mere appendages to a competing machine."

He believes these aggressive drivers fall prey to the illusion they are alone, disassociating themselves from others on the roadway. Because of this misconception, they think they are the masters of the road in their vehicles.

CHAPTER 17

So comes a reck'ning when the banquet's o'er,
the dreadful reck'ning, and men smile no more.
                                        —John Gay

When Mary Hill was arrested in April 2001, she was picked up at home by SCSO on the warrant issued by the state's attorney office. She was still having difficulty getting around and made the trip to the jail in a long black leather coat and wearing white bedroom slippers. SCSO agent Dan Risher, who served the warrant, contacted the jail and had a wheelchair waiting for her when they arrived there. She was booked, sitting in the wheelchair, but left after two hours, released on bond, leaning on the arm of attorney James Russ.

She returned to her reclusive existence in Wingfield North. Dennis Hill was busy hiring attorneys, preparing to win big against BMW. He hired Ted Culhane, Jr., a well-respected local defense attorney, to represent his wife. Then he hired Gerald Boyle, the Milwaukee defense attorney, well-known for defending serial killer Jeffrey Dahmer. Boyle was not licensed to practice in Florida, and was acting as an adviser.

The defense team was not the only team "working" the case. The Brevard-Seminole state attorney Norm Wolfinger and his office were staying in close contact with victims' families, the Browns, Stevens and the Rockwells.

They were all anxious for faster progress in the case, but as Wolfinger explained the process, they had to wait before making an arrest to be certain they had a provable case. Once the arrest was made, "the clock was ticking," and if a judge said, "We're going to trial tomorrow," then "we have to be ready," Wolfinger said. "That's why you don't want to make the arrest too soon. The clock is ticking once you do that. We like to get the case ready, so we can go immediately to court with the case, if necessary.

"I talked with the families a number of times myself, listening to their concerns. One thing they were concerned about was that after Jim Carter left, and Pat Whitaker became the felony intake supervisor and was going to prosecute the case, they felt he wasn't aggressive enough. I thought he was. Pat's a good prosecutor with lots of experience and worth a lot more than I pay him. I only had one concern, he was having a back problem and was going to need surgery. With Mrs. Brown and Mr. Stevens sitting with me, I called Pat and asked him if he felt he was up to the job, with all the pain he was having. He said he was.

"I said, 'That's it then, Pat's the man,' and he did a great job. Because of the complexity of the case, I added some assistants, Bart Schneider and Chris White, to help with the prosecution, and who could also step in if needed at any point. I know now, it was the right decision."

Before the trial would begin, depositions were taken from people expected to be called as witnesses. The car was examined numerous times by experts for both the defense and the prosecution. While all the background fact gathering was going on, the public was kept up to date by extensive media coverage. CBS's *48 Hours* came to town and began filming interviews for the episode they planned to air sometime in the future.

Before the case actually came to trial on Monday, February 23, 2004, Mary and Dennis Hill had already separated and were preparing for a nasty divorce case. Mary Hill fired the attorneys hired by Dennis Hill to defend her, and hired her own attorney, Timothy Berry. As a former BMW owner, he said he knew what could happen with the cruise control, and decided to retain the defense strategy formulated by Culhane and Boyle. Boyle would stick around for a while after Berry took over for the defense.

While the defense and prosecution teams were falling into place, there were problems in coming up with a judge to preside over the case. The fourth judge tagged for the job, O. H. Eaton Jr., became the presiding judge. He stepped in soon before the trial was to begin.

As the wheels of justice slowly turned, the day finally came when the trial would begin. It took nearly forty-three months from the time of the crash to the beginning of the trial. The trial would last one week, with the jury deliberating five hours before returning a verdict.

The jury was all female. The six jurors plus one alternate were all mothers, except for one. They all were employed in varied career fields: a Publix supermarket employee, a high school administrator, a pharmaceutical saleswoman, a computer specialist, a health care company manager and a bank employee. The alternate was a bookkeeper.

As impatient as the members of the victims' families—Rita and Jennifer Brown, Mel Stevens and Keith Rockwell, with his son and also victim, Zak Rockwell—were to see justice done, there were those who must have approached the first day of the trial with dread. Mary Hill, who had never believed she would be arrested for the crash, had not spoken to the Browns or Rockwells in all the time that had passed since the crash—not one word. She didn't call on the phone to express her sorrow about the death of Carrie or the injury of Zak. She didn't send a card. She didn't even send an e-mail. She didn't send a message to any of them asking them to come to her, while she couldn't drive—and when she could, she didn't drive the short distances to their homes to see them. Nothing, that's what they heard from Mary Hill. By the time the trial began, the Brown and Rockwell families wanted answers—they wanted justice—but most of all, they wanted Mary Hill to accept responsibility for what she had done.

The trial was held in the "old" Seminole County courthouse. It is a large, imposing edifice, with a sense of '50s- and '60s-style boxy architecture. The foundation is an unusual feature—a pyramidal concrete foundation that gives a bunker appearance to the building before it rises a few stories above the sidewalk. It is bordered along the front and back walkways, by moatlike reflecting pools. There are no fish, or animals of any type, nor aquatic plants, not even algae in them—they resemble pristine, shallow lap pools, protecting the foundation of the building from pedestrians who might want to touch it for some reason.

The wind blowing across Lake Monroe, which borders the north side of the building, keeps the huge

American flag in front of the building, alternately snapping in the wind or gently floating on the breezes. A street park lies between the lake and building. There is plenty of space to exercise and stretch legs cramped from sitting in the courtroom. There is beautiful scenery to ease the mind, after having it bombarded by continuous questioning or having tried to absorb lengthy testimonies.

The picturesque village of downtown Sanford wraps around the building and the municipal parking lot that is situated behind it. On-the-street parking is rapidly taken. The spaces in front of the building are snapped up by media trucks and vans, some arriving in the dark of early morning, to assure they get a prime vantage point, to catch impromptu sightings and interviews with the principals in the case as they enter and leave the building.

Many of the streets are red brick—the whole atmosphere surrounding the courthouse is one of old-town charm. The courthouse itself is the anachronism in the landscape. There are plenty of small restaurants and sandwich shops downtown, all within walking distance of the courthouse. Down the road, on US 17-92, all the familiar fast-food joints, which we all love, can be found—if you are willing to give up your parking space to travel to one. People who prefer to stroll around during their lunch break can window-shop antique stores and boutiques, or folks can simply enjoy the town's atmosphere while sitting on a park bench.

Regardless of how great a parking space you find, the bottleneck of the system is going through one of the security checkpoints. As more people arrive to participate in the daily activities of the courthouse, people queue up, waiting to place their briefcases, handbags and anything else they are carrying on a conveyor to be scanned for contraband by uniformed guards. Anyone other than badged personnel working or doing business in the courthouse must walk through a scanning door frame. If you are wearing metallic items that set off an alarm, you are scanned with a wand by one of the guards. It can be a time-consuming process, especially when many people arrive at the same time.

In the "old" courthouse, where the trial and most of the later hearings in the case were held, presiding judge O. H. Eaton held court in Courtroom B on the second floor. It had a relaxed feeling to it, with warm tones of wood and neutral tan and dark, muted yellow. It is a styling that brings back memories of the time when airport lobbies had seats of molded plastic chairs on stainless-steel pedestals, in alternating colors, but the courtroom had a more toned-down color spectrum than one would expect from an airport. The spectator seating curved around the back of the courtroom with comfortable theater-style chairs. There were no windows to give any clue to those in the courtroom as to what might be happening outside the building—whether rain clouds might be forming, or bright sunshine was warming the air, a comforting thought after sitting rigid in a frigid courtroom. To the people in Courtroom B, the only clue as to what was happening outside was during a recess when the huge glass windows in the courtroom waiting area hid nothing from view. The benches for waiting trial witnesses and prospective jurors were in this area.

The right side of the courtroom filled with family and friends of the victims and people interested in the case. The Browns, Rockwells, family and friends sat in the front rows behind the prosecution table. The numerous members of the press fitted themselves in, wherever they could. A still photographer from the *Orlando Sentinel* and a *48 Hours* cameraman acted as the press's eyes, preserving the images of the trial.

The only friend noted for defendant Mary Hill was Bob Roberts, a man who had worked for the Hills making repairs to their Wingfield North home, when they had moved from a few streets over, in the same community. He was known there, doing work for neighbors as well, and moved freely in and out of the development.

Roberts became a friend, and at one point, he was living in their pool house, giving rise to the moniker of "Cabana Boy," among some of the neighbors, but in a friendly, rather than derisive, tone. One observer in the neighborhood remembered seeing Dennis Hill and Roberts sitting in the driveway and drinking beers. He attended every day of the trial, including the sentencing hearings. He was the only apparent person to offer friendship and support to and for Mary Hill during the trial, other than her paid counsel team.

Roberts was the only person out of the hundreds of people Mary Hill certainly must have known, and some of whom she may have considered friends—often friends and acquaintances are confused—who showed up for her. None of the people she had done business with from her marketing firm, or the people whose businesses she had patronized, no neighbors or employees—not one of these people had come forward to offer her their support. She had spent the past $2\frac{1}{2}$ years isolating herself from everyone—she was a woman alone throughout the trial. According to Willis Towne, he knew a supervisor at Barbara Nolan who sent one of her trusted lieutenants as a trial observer. His job was to come back on a daily basis and tell her what was going on. But even he, on the Barbara Nolan Research Company payroll—her former company—wasn't there in the capacity of friend, only as a paid spy for another company employee.

The trial everyone had been waiting for was ready to begin. In the span of a week's time, the jury would hear opposing viewpoints and theories from the defense attorneys and prosecuting attorneys. They would be asked to listen to the testimony of expert witnesses, for both the defense and prosecution. Their subjects of expertise would range from crash scene analysis to automobile mechanics, especially in regard to cruise controls. They would hear from witnesses to the crash and to the erratic driving of Mary Hill as the crash occurred and prior to its happening. Among other witnesses would be a former Hill household employee and victim Zak Rockwell. Estranged husband Dennis Hill was also called upon to testify.

CHAPTER 18

Law is reason, free from passion.
                                    —Aristotle

As opening statements by opposing sides were given, ASA Bart Schneider would tell the jury that Mary Hill "was driving interstate speeds on a country road," preparing to discount any theories that her car was driving itself—he was making the point that she was driving, and driving fast.

Her defense attorney would tell the jury that his client "was neither homicidal nor suicidal" on that day. He was already anticipating the prosecution's move to show that client Mary Hill's mental-health problems were a contributing factor in the fatal crash. He was getting ready to place the groundwork for his theory, the event was just a tragic accident and that she was not at fault—the cruise control took over the car she was driving.

Prior to the trial, the defense team, through its many changes of attorneys, tried to obtain all the repair records for BMW cruise controls made at Field's BMW, the local dealership that serviced the

Hills' car. The management at Field's informed the court that it would be a nightmarish impossibility, as all their records would have to be examined individually, by hand, to try to find any such documents. The judge decided it wouldn't be feasible for the company to make the search, but did allow the defense team to subpoena information from corporate BMW—information readily available as computerized data at that level.

What was known was this: 410,000 BMWs were recalled by the automaker in 1992 through 1997 for faulty cruise control and throttle cable bushings. Among those models recalled was the 1996 740iL BMW—the same model Dennis Hill had purchased as a used automobile. A records search did indicate that the vehicle had been fixed during the recall, prior to Hill's purchasing the car.

BMW sent an expert witness to assist the prosecution, engineer Mark Yeldham, who works for its legal department. Yeldham told the court that BMW receives approximately fifty complaints a year of unplanned, sudden acceleration. After examining the Hill vehicle, he found no indication of mechanical error or that the car sped out of control on its own.

Prosecutor Pat Whitaker asked Yeldham: "You have no evidence at all that the cruise control was even on?"

Yeldham testified, "No." He told the court that there were "no faults stored in the car's computer." In his experience, he said, most complaints actually involved driver error.

The defense's BMW expert, Anthony F. Anderson, a British electrical engineer, showed a photo of a wire in the engine of the Hills' BMW. He blamed it for the alleged sudden acceleration—it displayed wear. He termed it "unreliable." He did say under

cross-examination that he had not found that the
cable had failed. "I don't know how it was working,"
Anderson said, "the day of the accident. Nobody
would know." His explanation of how the incident
could have occurred involved a road signal that could
give a false command to the car, causing a sudden acceleration event, a rogue command.

Defense crash expert Gary Stephens refuted the
conclusions of Corporal Wright's investigation report,
as well as the conclusions of state crash expert Hans
Fuehrer. Stephens was an accident reconstruction
specialist. It was his opinion, that Hill was going
through the curve at only sixty-seven and was only traveling at thirty-three–forty-two miles per hour when her
car collided with the tree.

Fuehrer, who examined road marks still visible at
the scene, seven months after the crash, was steadfast
in his belief that Hill was traveling through the curve
at seventy-three miles per hour, nearly forty miles
more than the recommended speed, and hit the tree
at approximately forty-five miles per hour. He found
nothing to question in Wright's crash report.

The jury listened to compelling testimony from
Jimmy Arthur and Stan Philpot, the men who saw the
crash occur and who were first on the scene. Their testimony about what had occurred prior to the crash
and immediately afterward would apparently make
a great impression on the women jurors.

Other BMW owners were called upon by the defense to relate their own problems with their vehicles
accelerating out of control.

When Dennis Hill was called to the witness stand,
jurors were not told that anything was out of the ordinary with the Hills' marriage. Prosecutor Pat Whitaker, however, was not taking any chances; Dennis Hill

might be a "loose cannon" who could possibly go anywhere in his testimony.

Pat Whitaker told the judge, out of the hearing of the jury, that "Mr. Hill is not exactly what I would call a cooperative witness, based upon the depositions that I've been involved with before. I'm afraid he's going to blurt out something like Mary Hill is a good driver. Mary Hill has no traffic offenses on her record [or about her] driving history, both of which would be inappropriate." (Actually, Mary Hill did have one speeding ticket on her Florida driving record.)

He asked the judge to "admonish him before he has the opportunity to do that in front of the jury. In other words, ask to have the jury taken out and have him instructed not to say those things. He has said those things unsolicited or in the depositions."

That admonishment was made to Hill, with the agreement of defense attorney Tim Berry. He wasn't taking any chances, either; loose cannons can roll anywhere on the deck. Neither attorney knew if Dennis Hill was the loose cannon who could damage the case for either of them. Judge Eaton asked Hill to "be careful about how you answer counsel's questions. Please, just answer the question that was asked. Don't try to make any speeches or make any side comments . . . or express any opinions that are not asked of you."

The judge told Hill if he slipped up and said something inappropriate that was bad enough, he would have to declare a mistrial. "We end up having to do this all over again," the judge said.

After asking some routine questions about his business and where he lived, and previous residences in the area, Whitaker asked Dennis Hill about the car. Hill told him he had purchased it used, a few years before (Whitaker was able to supply the exact year: 1998), and said it was registered in his name, although it was his wife's vehicle.

Hill was questioned about driving on Markham Woods Road, was able to supply the correct speed limit from memory, and knew that the distance from the intersection to his development was approximately half a mile. He said that it took him about five minutes of travel time between those two points.

He said he didn't drive Mary's car, even when they were traveling together. She would drive if they were in that vehicle. And, no, he said, he wasn't aware of any mechanical or operational defects or problems with the BMW "because Mary took care of her car because I was gone a lot, and when it needed service, she would take it in."

He told the court that he frequently picked up Kaitlynn from school. When he was in town, "I picked her up. When I wasn't, Mary would." He said that Amy "sometimes would take the bus and sometimes we'd pick her up," sharing those duties. "When I was in town, I'd pick her up, and when I wasn't here, Mary would pick her up."

Whitaker established a timeline with Dennis Hill for the events that occurred on August 7, 2000. Hill said he went straight from the house to work in the morning, returning back there in early afternoon, around 1:30 or 2:00 P.M., he wasn't sure of the specific time. It was the time, he said, he usually came home every day. (This time was an earlier time than Deane David recalled him coming home when she worked for the Hills.) After about a half hour, he left, driving his wife, Mary Hill, in her car, to a doctor's appointment.

Whitaker asked him why he was driving Mary's car. "I spend every day thinking why," said Hill, "because I never drove her car, ever. Why that day I drove her car, I don't know. I ask myself that every day. I don't know, because I have the slowest car in the world, and why I didn't take mine, I just don't know."

He said he drove them to a hospital located nearby that had doctor's offices adjacent to it. He estimated it took about twenty minutes to get there. He went in with her and met the doctor she was going to be consulting with. He knew that she was there to be evaluated to see if she needed ECT and that the doctor said it wasn't needed. He didn't know why. He figured they left the office at 3:30 P.M., which was just prior to Greenwood Lakes Middle School dismissal time. It took them about twenty minutes to drive from the doctor's office to the school.

When Whitaker asked him if he had any trouble with the vehicle driving to the hospital, he replied, "No, not at that time, no," agreeing that it seemed to be operating normally. He noticed nothing unusual in the drive to the school. After waiting about "five minutes or so," the kids were out of school.

After the kids got into the backseat, he drove to the Exxon station in Heathrow, experiencing no mechanical or operational problems with the car during the drive, driving traffic speed. "It wasn't anything fast, just whatever the traffic was doing. I was keeping up with traffic." He took the residential streets, never getting on the nearby interstate, to pick up a white Cadillac he had left at the station for repairs about a week prior. "I was gonna give it to somebody and I just wanted them to check it out, so it was just general maintenance," he told Whitaker.

After he got out of the BMW at the station, he went inside to confer with the station owner about the car being repaired. He saw his wife exit the passenger door, walk around the car, and get into the driver's seat. She then drove off. He wasn't aware of whether or not she put on her seat belt.

"Two or three minutes, four minutes, maybe five at the most," he said, he also left the station. He traveled the same route Mary Hill had, down International to Lake Mary Boulevard, through the intersection onto Markham Woods Road; then he saw the crash.

He testified there were no law enforcement officers on the scene at that time. He remembered seeing a couple of people there, but said they weren't rendering assistance, they were just standing there. "I checked the girls and I found no pulse."

When asked if his wife was there, his response was "Yeah. She was on the other side of the car." He said he checked her, too, and waited there at the scene until Zak Rockwell was taken away. He understood at the time "that they took him up to the station, and he was airlifted someplace. They took Mary at the same time."

Whitaker went back to the service station subject. "When Mary Hill left the Exxon station, did you notice anything about the way that she was driving when she left the parking lot?" he asked.

"No, sir" was Hill's reply.

"Did you have an occasion, one or two days after the crash, to meet a Corporal Wright, of the highway patrol?" Whitaker asked.

"Yeah. He brought by Amy's stuff that was in the car," which included her books and a book bag. They had a brief conversation at Hill's house at the time. He said he didn't recall telling Wright that Mary had left the Exxon station at a quicker than normal speed and that he was concerned.

When Berry questioned Hill, he asked him if he and his wife had any arguments or problems that day, if there was any difficulty between them on August 7, 2000. Hill said no.

Hill described her mood as being very good.

In redirect, Whitaker went straight to Mary Hill's mental state. "Mr. Hill, had Mary Hill had a problem with depression for quite some time?"

Hill asked him to repeat the question: "She had with what?"

"Had she had any problem with depression for quite some time?" Whitaker asked again.

"I don't believe so," Hill said.

"You know why she was going to get a second opinion for electroconvulsive therapy?"

"As far as I know," said Hill, "it's because it was recommended by the doctor that she had been going to."

"Do you know what that doctor's name is?"

"I think it was Suarez," he said.

Whitaker asked, "Was she taking medication for something, for depression?"

"Not at that time, no."

"You don't seem to know a whole lot about it, is that true?" Whitaker asked.

"That's true," Hill said. He was told by Judge Eaton that he could "step down from the witness stand. You're excused from attendance at court. Thank you for coming."

Dennis Hill left the courtroom.

As the attorneys questioned other witnesses, prodded for useful information and asked for recollections of anything that would be helpful, the case continued through the week. Finally, out of all the witnesses to take the stand, the person everyone in the courtroom had been waiting to hear from spoke. Mary Hill took the stand in her own defense. It was a dynamic moment of the trial when Tim Berry said, "The defense will call Mary Hill."

It was the moment so many people had been waiting for, for so long. They wanted Mary Hill to tell them what happened to their children, to their family members, to their friends. Zak Rockwell was waiting, too, to hear what the driver of the car had to say about what had happened the day his life changed forever.

The first words to pass Mary Hill's lips weren't the revelation the audience have been waiting for—they were simply a response to Mary Hill's greeting of her attorney. Her first words after almost forty-three months of dead silence were "Good morning."

"Miss Hill," Berry said, "I'm gonna ask you some questions about August 7, 2000, but I first need to ask you if you have a complete memory of those events of that day, or do you not remember some things?"

"I don't remember everything of that day, no." She responded to questions about where she had been, why and with whom. She told Berry that Dennis Hill had driven her to an afternoon appointment to see Dr. Gfeller in Sanford. She told him she felt fine after leaving the doctor's office. She then told him, "We went over to Greenwood Lakes Middle School (in Lake Mary) to pick up our daughter, and we parked over in the library and waited for her." The prosecution was having difficulty hearing her testimony and the judge prompted her to speak louder.

"After you picked the children up, where do you and Dennis go?" Berry asked.

"We went to the Exxon station, over by Heathrow, to pick up a car that was there for repair."

"And who picked up the car and who drove the children home?"

"He picked up the car and paid for it," Mary Hill said, "and we changed drivers and I drove everyone home."

"Now, do you remember anything out of the ordinary, anything unusual occurring on that trip from the gas station until you got to the intersection of Lake Mary and Markham Woods Road?"

"No, not really," she said.

"Do you remember almost sideswiping someone?"

"No."

"Do you remember seeing a white van?" Berry asked.

"Yes, I do." She told him in reply to the subsequent question, "I saw him parked, coming out of Heathrow as I drove by. I had the green light and I passed him, and he exited Heathrow and came over into the left lane and was behind me."

"Now, when you got to Markham Woods Road, do you remember if you had to stop for the traffic light, or was the light green for you to go on?"

"No, I stopped."

"Now, at the light, did you have any difficulty with your car at the light?"

"I really don't remember," she said.

"You don't remember if you had to back up?"

"No, I don't remember backing up."

Berry wanted to have her tell the court what happened at the time established as being the critical point in the incident, the beginning point of the one-tenth of a mile from the intersection at Lake Mary Boulevard to the oak tree next to Markham Woods Road that her car had crashed into. "Now, when the light changed, tell the jury what you did when you got the green light," he instructed her.

"I was . . . I made a left-hand turn, but I made the wide turn, I stayed to the right. Even though I was making a left, I was close to the curbside and—"

"Did something unusual happen in that turn?" he asked. "Tell us about that."

"As I started to come out of the turn," she said, "like where the curb ends, I felt my rear passenger tire kind of slide a little." She described the incident akin to hitting gravel or a patch of ice. "It just shimmied on me, and I wasn't in line with the front end."

She elaborated when he asked her if she tried to do anything to adjust for what had happened: "I let go of the accelerator and waited, thinking the car would right itself."

"What happened? What did the car do?"

"Accelerated," she said.

After more discussion in the courtroom about problems hearing her responses, she was asked to speak louder, "so we can all hear."

Berry asked her again, "When you took your foot off the gas, what happened? Did the car slow—did the car move forward—what happened?"

"It picked up speed," she said. "It started going faster."

"And then what did you do in response to the car gaining speed when you took your foot off the accelerator?"

"I applied the brake," she said.

"Okay. And what happened when you applied the brake?"

"Car kept going."

"What did you do then?"

"I released the brake and applied it again."

"What happened?"

"The car started to"—she faltered, then resumed—"the car started going out of the lane. It was fishtailing."

"And can you tell us, if you can, can you tell us what happened next?" Berry asked. "What are you doing? What are you thinking?"

"It happened very quickly," she said. "Everything was very quiet, and I just remember looking down at my dash, not at anything in particular. I didn't look at my odometer or anything, I just looked down at my dash. I said, 'Why won't you stop?'"

"To the car, you said, 'Why won't you stop?'"

"Yeah."

"What's the next thing you remember?" he asked.

"I woke up on the ground."

"During the time from [when] you felt that funny feeling with your wheel, were you trying to brake the car and slow the car?"

"Yes, I was."

"Did you ever intentionally accelerate and drive fast?"

"No," she said.

Pat Whitaker began his questioning of Mary Hill by inquiring about the car itself, where it had been earlier in the day, and determined from her answers that it had been parked in her driveway with the engine turned off. She described how they had taken residential roads and SR 434 to reach the doctor's office.

"Did you ever go onto any road where the cruise control would be engaged?" he asked.

"I wasn't driving the car. I don't know if he used it," she said.

He questioned her a little more about the streets they

had traveled down and the traffic; then Whitaker asked her if they went from the doctor's office to the school.

"Actually," she said, "we were early and we left the doctor's office because we were early, and Dennis went to a gas station and filled the car up and then we went back to the doctor's office."

"Okay. So he turned the engine off and filled the car up?" Whitaker inquired.

"Yes, he did."

He asked her about the roads going to the school, thus establishing they were primarily residential roads, not roads where you would engage cruise control.

She said, "No, I wouldn't."

Then he asked her about the trip from the school to the station and the type of roads they traveled; he inquired if they would be roads upon which you would engage the cruise control. She again said she wouldn't.

He questioned her about the traffic conditions. "And this being school-getting-out type of hour, three-thirty to four-thirty in the afternoon, it's fairly busy on the roads?" he asked.

"Yes, sir," she said. "School buses, traffic."

He asked her if she had taken over the car at the Exxon station; to which she replied she did. He asked, "And you drove out normally from that station?"

"Excuse me?"

"You drove out normally from that station?" he asked again.

"Yes, sir."

"Had no problems with the car?"

"No."

"And your husband hadn't had any problems with the car?"

"No."

"And did you engage the cruise control?"

"Ah, no, sir, I did not," she said, "but there's . . . The button that activates my cruise control on the dash was on mostly all the time."

"Had you turned it on?"

"It was always on. There wasn't, it wasn't necessary to turn it on and off," she said.

"Okay. Just let me ask the question," he said. "That's the answer? Okay. So you say it was always on?"

"I believe so."

"You had been driving this car for several months, is that right?" he asked.

"Um, probably, like, two years," she said.

He quizzed her about the speed limits in the area of the crash. She knew them all, including the warning about the suggested speed of thirty-five miles per hour for the curve. "How many times had you been through that intersection?"

"Thousands," she said.

"This crash occurred August 7, 2000?"

"Yes, sir."

"And there was an investigation that continued on from that crash for a good number of months, is that correct?"

"Yes, sir," she said.

"Were you aware of that?"

Mary was shaking her head yes, and Whitaker advised her she had to say the answer out loud. Although he could see her answer, she needed to say it.

"I did. Yes, sir."

"Did you tell any of the investigators that were handling the crash investigation that this had happened, what you said here today in the courtroom?"

She told him she didn't understand the question. Whitaker tried another approach. "All right. This morning in the courtroom, you talked about the car accelerating, is that right?"

"Yes, sir."

"On its own, is that correct?"

"Yes, sir."

"During the months of that investigation that you knew was going on, did you tell any investigators that that happened?"

"No investigator talked to me," she said.

"You knew there was an investigation going on, is that correct?"

"Yes, sir."

"You knew that your driving was the subject of that investigation, is that correct?"

"Yes, sir."

At this point, Berry interrupted with an objection, telling Judge Eaton, "After six days, we are now coming dangerously close to commenting on her right to remain silent, and she was silent on the advice of her lawyers, and I am just so afraid that we're gonna trip over that somehow."

Whitaker told the judge, "I'm almost completely finished with it. It's prearrest silence in an investigation. It's admissible, but I'm almost done. I'm not gonna hardly ask any more questions."

When Judge Eaton allowed the proceedings to resume, Whitaker asked, "Do you recall having a conversation several months after the crash? Do you know who Deane or Deane David is?"

"Yes, sir, I do."

"And how do you know her?"

"She worked for me prior as a housekeeper and helped with the girls, taking them to their dance and piano lessons."

When Whitaker said he was having difficulty

hearing her responses, she said, "I'm sorry, I don't talk very loud."

"Do you recall her calling you several months after the crash?" he asked.

The defense objected, saying this was asking for hearsay evidence, but Bart Schneider and Pat Whitaker pointed out the state had just asked about a conversation, not the content of it. The judge allowed the questioning to continue.

"Okay," said Whitaker. "Once again, do you recall Deane David calling you on the telephone several months after the crash?"

"No, I do not remember that."

"Do you recall having any conversations with Deane David after the crash?"

"I saw her at Amy's funeral."

"Do you recall any other conversation with her, besides at the funeral?"

"No, I do not."

"Do you recall telling Deane David that you didn't remember what happened in the crash?"

"No, I don't remember talking to her after the crash."

"And you had no problems with your vehicle going down Lake Mary Boulevard and stopping at the traffic light at Lake Mary Boulevard and Markham Woods Road?"

"No, sir."

"And you say you stopped there, normally?"

"I don't know what the question . . . I came to the light and I stopped."

"You don't remember the car backing up?"

"No, I don't remember that."

"You don't recall stopping with your nose . . . your car beyond the stop bar?"

"No, sir, I don't remember that."

"As you go down Markham Woods Road, are there side streets leading off into neighborhoods from that road before you get to that intersection to your subdivision?"

"Yes, sir."

"Do you recall putting your seat belt on?"

"No, I did not have my seat belt on."

"And previous . . . you had had no previous problems with the car accelerating or with the cruise control, is that correct?"

"None that warranted saying anything about. I didn't perceive them as a problem. I thought there were times when I did use the cruise control that I would set it at fifty and it would jump a little bit more and I brought it down. I thought that was normal, but nothing major."

"Nothing that you took the car in to have it repaired for, is that correct?"

"Right."

"How would the kids usually get home from school?"

"Sometimes they would take the bus, sometimes one of the parents would pick them up, they would get a ride."

"How, I guess my question was, how would they usually get home from school?"

"I just answered that," she said. "If there was a parent there, they would . . . We all lived in the same neighborhood, they would come home together, or [if] the parent wasn't available, then they came home on the bus."

"So you weren't usually the person who picked them up?"

"I picked them up quite often. My husband picked

them up quite often. Mrs. Brown picked them up. Zak's dad."

Whitaker then took her back through the sequence of things happening from the time she left the intersection at Markham Woods Road, asking if she was accelerating rapidly. She said no she wasn't, that she accelerated from a stop, not going around a turn. As he received information from her that the car was lunging, going faster and faster on its own, he inquired about whether or not she braked as the car was continuing to accelerate.

"Surely at this point you pressed on the brakes, is that right?" he asked.

"No, sir, not right then."

"And surely real quick after that you pressed on the brakes?"

"Yes, I did."

"And you pressed really hard on those brakes?"

"No, sir, I did not."

"You did not press hard on the brakes?"

"No, I did not floor it."

"You felt the car accelerating and you weren't pressing the accelerator and you didn't push hard on the brakes?"

"I didn't want the brakes to lock and my rear tire was still not acting—I didn't want to lock my rear tire, I thought."

"That car," Whitaker said, "you know what ABS braking system is?"

"Yes, sir."

"Do you know what the purpose is?"

"Antilock brakes."

"So they will not lock," he asked.

"So they say."

Whitaker paused for a short time before asking,

"Miss Hill, you've sat here through the testimony in this entire trial, is that correct?"

"Yes, sir."

"And you heard Mr. Arthur, James Arthur testify, is that right?"

She acknowledged that she had, but when Whitaker asked her if she had nearly sideswiped him with her car, her reply was "Absolutely not."

She said the events that he had said happened did not occur. The only part of his testimony that she did agree with was that at some point they were both traveling on Lake Mary Boulevard at the same time, and that James Arthur was directly behind her at the traffic light.

When Pat Whitaker turned the witness, Mary Hill, back over to Tim Berry, Berry asked her about Deane David. He asked her if she had once been an employee, and Mary Hill said yes, and that she had terminated her.

Berry asked her about what happened after the crash.

"At some point during this accident, or immediately thereafter, did you become unconscious?"

"Yes," she said. "I woke up after I was thrown from the vehicle. I woke up on the ground." At his prompting, she continued. "I felt intense heat. I thought I was on fire and I rolled in my sweater to get away from the engine and to be able to get back to the car and to get to the kids, but I started falling back."

"Was the car still running?" he asked.

"Yes."

"What kind of car did you learn to drive in?"

"Excuse me?"

"What kind of car did you learn to drive in?" he repeated.

"My first car was a Firebird."

"What year?"

"Probably a '66."

"You didn't have antilock brakes that you remember?"

"No."

And that was all that the people who had waited so long for answers heard from Mary Hill. The jury would deliberate five hours, on that same day, Saturday, February 28, 2004, to return a verdict of guilty on two counts each of vehicular homicide and manslaughter; count 5, the negligence charge, was dismissed.

When she heard the verdict, she closed her eyes and said, "I'm going to jail."

Over the prosecution's protest, Judge Eaton allowed her to go home, still on bond, although she had to relinquish her driver's license, which the state had restored. A sentencing date was set for April 16, 2004.

Afterward, Mary Hill was escorted through the crowd gathered outside the courthouse. Rita Brown told the media surrounding her, "Carrie got her day in court." She told the reporters pressing in toward the family, "I still feel numb. You can't take away the ache, the pain, the hurt, [but] we can go forward now. I prayed and hoped that justice would come and it came today."

Keith and Zak Rockwell were equally pleased with the outcome of the verdict.

Florida uses a point system for sentencing guidelines. Different factors are taken into consideration. The state guideline for Mary Hill's conviction suggested twenty-one years' imprisonment on the low end and thirty years' imprisonment on the high end.

CHAPTER 19

Happiness depends upon ourselves.
                                        —Aristotle

   Allowed to go free after the verdict on February 28, 2004, Mary Hill returned to her Wingfield North home. She was still alone, still unhappy, and now she didn't have daughters Jennifer, Amy or Kaitlynn to give her support and comfort. She had no support from husband Dennis—emotional or financial. Their relationship had become so acrimonious that her divorce lawyer, Mark Fromang, of Orlando, was busy filing motions and pleas with family court, trying to get Dennis Hill to pay the court-ordered payments for the household, the vehicle and insurance payments. Plus, he was being pushed for the support payments he was supposed to be paying. Fromang was answering Dennis Hill's counterpleas and motions as well. Times were just getting dismal. The situation was becoming ugly.
   When April 16 rolled around, everyone was once again in Judge Eaton's courtroom, expecting to hear a sentence handed down by the court for Mary Hill.

There was a major surprise. The shocking news was the sentencing would be delayed.

At the proceeding, the defense team told Judge Eaton that their client needed residential treatment and community control. They told him that prison couldn't provide the treatment she required for her mental and physical problems. And a bombshell was dropped: a psychiatrist told the judge that Mary Hill was suicidal.

Dr. Walter Afield, defense psychiatrist, told Judge Eaton that Mary Hill needed "immediate, extensive, long-term treatment, or you'll have a dead lady on your hands." Judge Eaton would say after the actual sentence was imposed in July that the statement had a great impact on his decision to delay sentencing. Dr. Afield was very emphatic that Mary Hill was suicidal and would kill herself if sent to prison.

The state maintained that the situation couldn't be that serious, or why hadn't she sought treatment since the crash? Why now? The state prosecution's position was that her reckless driving was not a onetime occurrence, but continued after the crash. Her reckless driving and endangerment of daughter Kaitlynn had been one of the reasons the state took Kaitlynn away from her. Alexis Hartzell, a teenager and former neighbor, who moved from her parents home and was taken in by Mary Hill for a while after the crash, said she witnessed Mary Hill putting alcohol in a water bottle, then drinking it while she was driving. She had been a passenger in a vehicle with Mary Hill driving out of control. "Nothing I said, or Kaitlynn said, would make her slow down." Mary was angry for some unknown reason and was speeding, weaving in and out of traffic. "I told her to slow down. I started crying. She was really angry," said Alexis.

* * *

The victims' families were allowed to address the court during this hearing. Keith Rockwell told Judge Eaton, "It is so frustrating to do everything right and then have someone's reckless act ruin everything." He told of his heartache and how he had suffered, wondering if his son, Zak, would ever come out of the coma the crash had left him in.

Rita Brown told the court, "A mother is not supposed to bury her child. It is not the way things were intended to be. Now I must turn my attention to the woman who sits before you. It is my belief that she must be held accountable for her actions and there is no sentence that you can impose, that will balance those scales."

Judge Eaton said, "This is one of the most difficult cases I've been assigned to" in his seventeen years on the bench. He decided to allow another psychiatric evaluation of Hill before imposing sentence.

After Tim Berry asked permission of the court for his client to speak, a tearful Mary Hill finally apologized, with a slightly shaky voice, saying, "The words 'I'm sorry' can never convey to her how I feel. I do apologize to the parents and to the families and to the friends and to everyone that knew Carrie and Amy and Zak. Amy and Carrie were best friends—they went everywhere together. They relied on each other. I just pray they are together now."

Hill was put in the custody of the Seminole County Jail, where she was placed on around-the-clock suicide watch by jail officials. A new sentencing date was set for May 10, 2004.

After the hearing, Keith Rockwell told reporters that he was confident the judge would follow the guidelines that called for a twenty-one-year prison sentence. Zak Rockwell said of Mary Hill's apology, "It was too little, too late, I guess."

Rita Brown told reporters she did accept her apology, "but she still has to be accountable."

Although she hadn't been sentenced to prison this day, the new development in the case caused a decided downward turn in Mary Hill's life. If she wasn't depressed before, her new situation would certainly make anyone depressed.

Being on suicide watch in Seminole County Jail was not a pleasant prospect. The inmate was kept under twenty-four-hour surveillance in a stripped-down cell with no amenities, wearing only one garment. It closely resembled a quilted furniture-moving pad, rolled into a cylinder, with wide straps over the shoulders to hold it on the inmate's body. (The jail trustees don't want inmates killing themselves while in their custody.) Inmates, not afforded even the least bit of privacy, must be miserable and humiliated if they are not as depressed as they were thought to be.

The issue of mental health, which the defense team worked to keep out of the trial, now became their focal point in trying to keep Mary Hill from being sent to prison.

The May 10 sentencing was delayed because the new mental evaluation had not been made. A new date of June 3, 2004, was set.

Mary Hill got a wonderful gift, though—basically a get-out-of-jail-free card. On Thursday, May 17, Judge Eaton ruled she could go to Shands Psychiatric Hospital, the prestigious teaching hospital connected to the University of Florida, to be evaluated if doctors there would admit her. The court allowed her to be placed in the custody of attorney Tim Berry, to be taken to a mental hospital of her choice, for evaluation. They were to prepare a report to be given to the court, assessing her mental condition. Mary Hill selected Shands at Vista, in Gainesville, Florida. She would be a patient in the hospital until the necessary testing and evaluations were completed.

The June 3 hearing was also postponed, as Hill was still undergoing psychiatric evaluation at Shands. The doctors there had yet to supply a copy of their mental-health evaluation to the prosecutors. This was the third sentencing delay within a two-month period. The victims' families were beside themselves with frustration and anguish. It seemed the defense team wanted to convince the judge that a downward sentence was appropriate, a really downward sentence. They wanted him to sentence Mary Hill to undergo inpatient psychiatric treatment, followed by house arrest instead of prison time.

On Friday, July 9, the state prosecutors asked for an emergency hearing. The judge would hear it on Thursday, July 15, early in the morning before another hearing already on his schedule. Pat Whitaker had learned that Mary Hill was not in the hospital at Shands. She was hospitalized only for a period of three weeks, then began treatment on an outpatient basis. A private investigator, working for a victim's family, discovered Mary Hill's location after the state had broken the news to the Browns and Rockwells that Mary Hill was not in Shands, as everyone had thought. Whitaker didn't know where she was, all he knew was that she wasn't a patient in the hospital when called there.

Rita Brown decided she wanted to know where

the woman convicted of killing her daughter Carrie was now residing. Obviously, she wasn't in jail on suicide watch. She wasn't in a mental hospital undergoing evaluation. She had to be somewhere. The investigator found that Mary Hill was staying in a luxurious, gated-apartment complex, Legacy Apartments, with another mental-health patient as a roommate. There was no hospital supervision. In fact, there was no direct supervision of any kind; it was an apartment complex, pure and simple, where the hospital leased space for outpatient housing use.

At the hearing, Tim Berry, Hill's attorney, told the court that she was not free to come and go as she pleased. She had to attend therapy groups and report for treatment sessions. She was only allowed off the grounds of the resortlike complex in the company of another mental-health patient or to go to the hospital for treatment.

Rita Brown and Mel Stevens were at the hearing, showing printouts of the amenities of the apartment complex, which included, among other things, a swimming pool, tennis court and fitness center. It showed large, beautifully decorated apartments.

Pat Whitaker asked that Mary Hill be returned to the Seminole County Jail. He was outraged that instead of being in jail under the suicide watch that seemed to be called for, or as a patient in the hospital under the supervision of mental-health professionals, she had been living free and living large, on her own, for more than a month.

Monica Guidry, the hospital's outpatient manager, told the court that the hospital leased several apartments in the complex for the use of its outpatient business.

She testified Hill did have at least one roommate, another mental-health patient. She said that Hill cannot come and go as she pleased. She was not allowed to drive—although she could ride with other patients who had vehicles and could drive—and she could not go anywhere without asking permission. (Of course, there was no one there to ask permission of, except her roommate, who was also undergoing treatment. There was no supervision by hospital administrators or employees of patients lodging in the luxury apartment complex.) Guidry said Hill spent most of her days and evenings at the hospital, undergoing treatment. She said the outpatients had to check in to the treatment program several times a week.

Whitaker considered Hill a flight risk, seeing that she might be sentenced to thirty years in prison. He asked she be brought back to the county's detention center.

Judge Eaton told the prosecutor, "There's not one scintilla of evidence that that's the case," allowing her to stay, undergoing treatment, until the newly set sentencing date arrived.

The sentencing date became a problem. The judge offered dates open on his schedule, all of them were while Rita Brown was scheduled to be in Greece for the upcoming Olympics, assisting the gymnastics team, except for a date in September. After hurried conferencing, Pat Whitaker selected a date in late summer, September 9. It was the only date that allowed Brown to be in attendance. Emotion at this point was riding high in the courtroom; then Brown burst out in anger and frustration that the sentencing would be more than four years after the date of her daughter's death.

Outside the courtroom the media eagerly encircled

Brown and Stevens as they held up the color flyer of the apartment complex where Hill was staying.

"She is not being treated for anything but alcohol and depression," Brown told reporters, "and I'm more depressed than she is right now, because our system is terrible, ridiculous, and I could cry. That's how angry I am," and she was close to tears. She said if Mary Hill, after the accident, had come as a neighbor and said how sorry she was about what had happened, no one would be here today. Nothing would have taken place, but she saw no remorse in this woman for what she had done.

Adding fuel to the already inflamed situation, Fox Network's Bill O'Reilly, the host of *The O'Reilly Factor*, entered into the volatile situation. He features an ongoing segment on his show entitled "Bad Judges." He boasts to viewers that he was responsible for one "bad judge" being taken off the bench, and there will be others.

On one show, he berated Judge Eaton, regarding an earlier Seminole County case. It was a case where a lot of people disagreed with the sentence he gave. It involved a teenage girl, a boy just into adulthood and a sticky situation, where all was not what it seemed on the surface. Taking everything he was aware of into consideration, he gave the young man a lighter sentence than the guidelines dictated. It really was not a popular sentence, and O'Reilly went after the judge. The show's producers had already scheduled Rita Brown to be interviewed about what was happening in regard to Mary Hill, when former-President Ronald Reagan died. His weeklong funeral coverage preempted the show on which the interview was to take place.

After the July 15 hearing, though, Brown told reporters that she was leaving the courthouse and was

immediately going to call O'Reilly's producers, she
wanted this judge off the bench.

An opening on the judge's schedule allowed for the
sentencing to be moved up, and a new sentencing
date (the fifth one in the case) was set. The new date
would be Friday, July 30, 2004. It would allow Rita
Brown to travel to the Olympics, knowing the fate of
the woman who killed her daughter. It would hopefully give the Rockwells a chance to put this episode
behind them and get on with the business of living.

It seemed nothing in this case was simple. Tim
Berry placed an ad in the Thursday, July 29, 2004, edi-
tion of the *Orlando Sentinel*, begging a mystery witness
to come forward. He stated a woman named "Darlene" had called his office more than once to relate
information that Mary Hill could use in a verdict
appeal. She wouldn't reveal her name, he wasn't able
to trace the call and she didn't keep an appointment
they made to discuss the information she knew. He
said he had trouble even getting the *Orlando Sentinel*
to accept the ad, which they finally did, after he
made a copy change at their request. The mysterious
Darlene didn't appear in court the next day, although
the ad ran. (It would be apparent a few months later
why she didn't respond.)

The night before the hearing, Zak Rockwell and
friends held a vigil ceremony at the memorial tree on
Markham Woods Road, the site of the car crash that
killed his friends Carrie Brown and Amy Hill, and
caused him grave injury. He wanted to honor Carrie
and Amy's memory.

Rita Brown had been busy sending e-mails to
people in the community, asking them to overfill

Courtroom B the next day, to pressure Judge Eaton to sentence Hill to prison.

The day of sentencing arrived and everyone was back in Courtroom B again. Mary Hill, free in Berry's custody, sashayed into the courtroom looking the best anyone had seen her look in court. She was much slimmer. She wore a mandarin-collared, silk- or satin-finished, pastel-flowered jacket, with a white background, and a black pencil skirt. The ensemble had a high-fashion flair. She was wearing simple jewelry, some bracelets, a watch and a ring. Her makeup was softer, and her hair was worn in a loose, flowing style, with ashy tones, instead of the brassier gold of her previous hairstyles. It was all very flattering to her. She was looking good, and she acted as though she knew it. She moved around the courtroom freely, talking with members of the defense team, with ever-faithful Bob Roberts and her daughters, Jennifer and Kaitlynn, who had driven over from Lake County, to give support to their mom. She exuded confidence. She walked around the courtroom, and in the corridor, like a woman who was expecting her freedom to be given to her.

Her divorce attorney had answered a motion filed by Dennis in the divorce case, where Dennis was wanting the marital residence back and the cars, as he was assuming that she wouldn't need any of those things while in prison. Fromang filed a countermeasure on her behalf, seemingly indicating that his client thought she *would* be needing those things. He cited the possibility of her not being sentenced to prison, but rather to a form of house arrest or probation with treatment. It was the ultimate in optimism . . . perhaps the mental-health treatment was working for Mary.

There was an edge to the atmosphere in the

courtroom, almost as if everyone was expecting the unexpected—whatever that might be. A still photographer from the *Orlando Sentinel,* acting as the pool photographer, was set up in the jurors' box, with the cameraman from *48 Hours.* The show hadn't been in attendance for the numerous hearings that had been taking place. Press members almost outnumbered everyone else in attendance.

At one point, after the proceeding began, an overwrought Kaitlynn ran out of the courtroom. Zak Rockwell, who was sitting across the aisle behind the prosecution, slipped out of the courtroom after her, presumably to comfort her. They both returned in short order. There was a near-capacity crowd on the prosecution side of the room. Almost no one was seated on the defense side—mostly defense team members and press. Dennis Hill quietly slipped in with a young man, probably in his late twenties or early to mid-thirties, who resembled him, especially in coloring. They sat down a few rows in back of Jennifer and Kaitlynn, to the outside of the aisle.

Dr. William Whitman, a psychiatrist with the Florida Department of Corrections (FDC), explained to the court the different types of mental-health treatment available in the Florida prison system. He carefully explained the degrees of depression, and how and where different levels would be treated by the system's health care professionals. If Hill was sentenced to prison, he thought Lowell Correctional Institute, in nearby Marion County, would be a good consideration, as it would place Hill closer to her family. If she needed greater treatment than available at Lowell, he thought the next best prison in the system would be Homestead Correctional Institute, at the southern end of the state.

* * *

When Judge Eaton addressed the court the collective intake of breath was audible. It was apparent to everyone that he intended to hand down a prison sentence—not probation and house arrest, as the rumor mill had suggested. Speculation had been rampant for days.

Judge Eaton was careful to explain how he had arrived at the sentence he was going to impose. He pointed out, how he knew all about the speculation that was being bandied about in the community, and could understand the frustrations of the victims' families and the surviving victim. Although he came to the case late, as the fourth judge assigned to it, and quickly had to familiarize himself with the case, the prosecution and defense had worked on it for years. He thought that situation may have been the source of some impatience with him. Early on, he had thought the state sentencing guidelines would total up to a substantial sum—although he was emphatic in pointing out that he had not prejudged the case, as some people had accused.

Judge Eaton said he "bent over backward to give Hill an opportunity to be heard—when mental issues were raised," yet he felt all along that "Hill should pay for her crimes."

Judge Eaton sentenced Mary Hill to fifteen years in prison and five years' probation, denying her the privilege of operating a motor vehicle during the probationary period.

After the sentencing, Rita Brown said, "I questioned at times who was the victim in this case. It seemed like he (Judge Eaton) was leaning toward the victim being Mary Hill and not the actual victims—

the girls themselves. But, today, he explained that. He was very detailed, he had a reason for that, and he satisfied my curiosity and my questions and he did it very well." She explained her about-face on her recent opinions of the judge. "I was pleased with what I heard today, and he brought it to layman's terms to everybody there. I think we are all satisfied with the outcome. He remembered the girls—they are the true victims."

Judge Eaton did remember the girls, saying, "There is no getting around two wonderful people are dead. . . . The court's position has been since the verdict came in to this very day that a substantial prison sentence was the proper resolution of this case."

When reporters asked Zak Rockwell what he thought about the sentence, he told them, "It happened today, what we were hoping for, a just sentence. I think it's the right amount of time—enough for her to reflect and see what she did." He told other reporters, "I can see it coming from her daughters (their reactions), how hard it is to see their mom in handcuffs, and for that, I do feel sympathy, but she had it coming. It represents justice for friends killed."

Mary Hill's husband—whom some in the media were erroneously calling her ex-husband—was involved in two volatile confrontations in the courtroom after the sentencing. Dennis Hill, seated a few rows back from Jennifer Wilson and Kaitlynn, leaped up as Kaitlynn became distraught when her mother was being handcuffed to be led away. He came up from behind Kaitlyn and attempted to embrace her, but she pulled away from him, rebuffing the gesture. He looked both hurt and confused, then lashed out verbally at Jennifer, accusing her of being the cause of Kaitlynn's reaction to him.

He stalked back to the area where he had been seated, where the man he had arrived with was waiting. Hill was clenching and unclenching his fists. His face turning red and purplish, his gaze fell on a man at the end of the row by the outside wall. He rushed over to the man, Tim Berry's son, Mike, also an attorney, with clenched fists down to his side, using very strong language, accusing him of being "the cause of all this." The reason for his anger may never be known, as Dennis Hill isn't talking to the media. Berry later laughed off the situation.

Bailiffs descended on him from the back of the courtroom and forced him to sit down, hands poised above his shoulders, to push him back down if he attempted to rise from the seat. Other bailiffs advised Mike Berry to leave the courtroom, which he did, before they allowed Hill to leave.

Finally exiting the courtroom, an angry Dennis Hill delivered his parting shot at reporters: "I will be glad when they hang up the sign that says, 'Rita Brown Courthouse.'"

When Mary Hill was led off by a female bailiff in waist chain and handcuffs, she told the girls, "I'll be okay."

She was driven over to the Seminole County Jail, to again be placed on suicide watch until her departure for prison, in about a week's time.

Although sentenced to fifteen years' prison time, she could possibly be released after serving 85 percent of the sentence, twelve years and nine months. Age fifty-three at the sentencing, Mary Hill could not hope to get out of prison until she was sixty-six years old, unless her attorneys could get the sentence overturned. Mary Hill was a woman who, even in reduced circumstances, was living a life of privilege. Instead of living in a mansion or a luxury apartment, she was now confronted with the proposition of living in a sixty-room dormitory, her only privacy allowed for some personal hygiene.

No longer would she be able to get into a red Mercedes convertible and go shopping on a whim. She would be living in an extremely controlled environment . . . a place where the lights were turned off at 10:00 P.M., regardless of whether or not she wanted to retire at that time. No more expensive facials, manicure and pedicures would be available to her. She could purchase and wear makeup, but would not be allowed to color her hair. Beautiful designer clothes and expensive jewelry would be a thing of the past; a prison uniform would become her fashion statement—a statement with no individuality, it would be the same worn by every other inmate in the prison. Mary Hill was going to a maximum-security women's prison, where she would be given psychiatric treatment as needed, until she was well enough to fit in and work in prison.

Judge Eaton told her, "Mary Hill, I don't know what you are going to do with your life. You are going to have to make a lot of adjustments. You are going to have to make a determination about what you are going to be able to do in order to try to better yourself and perhaps an opportunity to better those around you."

In his sentencing departure order, Judge Eaton succinctly narrated the whole case in a very understandable manner and explained *how* he arrived at the imposed sentence and *why*.

The following excerpted version, with footnotes and case references deleted, explains the case very well. Judge Eaton wrote in his *Sentencing Departure Order:*

The defendant was convicted by a jury of two counts of manslaughter and two counts of

vehicular homicide arising out of a tragic automobile accident that occurred on August 7,
2000. The evidence at trial established that the
defendant was driving erratically while approaching from the east toward the intersection
of Lake Mary Boulevard and Markham Woods
Road. She stopped her vehicle at the intersection but the front tires on the vehicle were
beyond the stop line. When the signal light
changed to allow her to proceed, she turned left
and accelerated to a speed of nearly 70 miles
per hour, lost control of her vehicle and crashed
into a tree, killing two of the three children
riding with her and seriously injuring the third.
One of the children who died was her own
daughter. The other was her daughter's best
friend. The defendant was thrown from the
vehicle and received serious injuries, including
a head injury.

The defendant's counsel attempted to show at
trial that the vehicle, a BMW, accelerated on its
own due to mechanical failure, but no direct evidence of mechanical failure was offered, although
there was some speculation about it. The defense
expert did not convince the jury that he found mechanical problems with the vehicle and the most
convincing part of his testimony was his opinion
that the circumstances of the accident tended to
exclude any other possibility. Other witnesses testified that they had experienced difficulties with
their BMW'S [sic], but their experiences were not
proven to be related to the mechanical difficulties
claimed by the defendant.

The defendant testified and claimed that the
vehicle got away from her and suddenly accelerated. The jury did not believe her and the
other evidence in the case refutes her statement.

Probably she is "in denial" about what happened just prior to the accident, but there is evidence that her injuries have interfered with her memory and that may also contribute to her inability to recollect events.

Under Florida law, a person cannot be convicted of both manslaughter and vehicular homicide for the death of the same victim. The court, therefore, at the suggestion of the prosecutor, adjudicated the defendant to be guilty of one count of vehicular homicide (Count II) and one count of manslaughter (Count III) and scheduled a sentencing hearing on April 16, 2004.

At the hearing, Dr. Walter Afield, a respected psychiatrist, testified that the defendant was suffering from profound depression and was presently suicidal. He recommended that she be admitted for immediate treatment at Shands Hospital in Gainesville, Florida. Dr. Debra Day, a psychologist who is well known to the court, expressed the same opinion as Dr. Afield. Based upon this expert testimony, the court remanded the defendant to custody and the sheriff placed her on suicide watch. She was subsequently released from custody to be admitted to Shands Hospital where she has been treated on both an inpatient and an outpatient basis.

The presumptive sentence in this case is in excess of twenty years imprisonment in the Department of Corrections. Defense counsel has argued that there is justification for a downward departure from the presumptive sentence.

In order to determine whether a downward departure is appropriate, the court must utilize a two step process. The first step is to determine whether a valid basis for departure is supported by the facts by the greater weight of the evidence.

If so, the second step is for the court to consider whether a departure is the best sentencing option for the defendant by weighing the totality of the circumstances in the case, including any aggravating or mitigating factors.

The court agrees that a downward departure is appropriate in this case for the reasons stated herein. However, the court does not agree that both of the reasons presented by the defendant justify a departure. In particular, the court finds that justification for a downward departure because "the defendant requires specialized treatment for a mental disorder that is unrelated to substance abuse or addiction or for a physical disability, and the defendant is amenable to treatment" is not supported by the evidence. The court is convinced that the defendant's mental health problems are related to addiction, thereby disqualifying her from a departure on this ground. Fortunately, the defendant has responded to treatment at Shands Hospital and is in much better mental health today than she was previously. Furthermore, the evidence establishes that the Department of Corrections can provide the treatment she needs in the future.

There are other reasons that justify a downward departure.

The offense was committed in an unsophisticated manner and was an isolated incident for which the defendant has shown remorse:

The legislature has provided for the court to depart from the presumptive sentence if the offense was committed in an unsophisticated manner and was an isolated incident for which the defendant has shown remorse. Sophistication may be in the eye of the beholder but the facts of this case do not show the defendant to have operated her motor vehicle in a sophisticated manner. In fact, the evidence is otherwise. The court, therefore, finds that the offenses for which she has been convicted were committed in an unsophisticated manner.

The evidence also establishes that she has shown remorse. She has remained in virtual seclusion since the date of the accident and has expressed remorse to her husband and to Dr. Afield. She has mourned the loss of the children to [*sic*] and was depressed to the point of being suicidal. And while she did not express an apology to the families of the other victims in the case until the sentencing hearing, remorse can be expressed without an apology.

At the trial and at the sentencing hearing the court recognized the deep sorrow and depression displayed by the defendant. There were times when the trial had to be interrupted because the defendant simply could not continue listening to the testimony. While the defendant experienced depression prior to August 7, 2000, the "profound, overwhelming, severe depression" described by Dr. Afield was manifested after the accident. This condition is not usually present in defendants who are simply sorry they have been caught up in the criminal justice system. Additionally, the defendant directly expressed her remorse at the sentencing hearing and apologized for her actions. Finally, as the sentencing score sheet shows, the defendant has no prior record of causing accidents or committing other crimes.

The capacity of the defendant to appreciate the criminal nature of the conduct or to conform that conduct to the requirements of law was substantially impaired:

For the last century or so, the law has recognized the special problems inherent in imposing criminal responsibility upon defendants who have mental problems. For instance, insane persons are not held accountable for their criminal acts. However, in Florida, mental health problems short of insanity do not excuse criminal conduct. Because of the special problems associated with sentencing persons with mental illness, the legislature has provided not one, but two, reasons authorizing downward departures from the presumptive sentence when mental issues are presented. In addition to the departure for specialized treatment already mentioned, the legislature has authorized a downward departure when "the capacity of the defendant to appreciate the criminal nature of the conduct or to conform that conduct to the requirements of law was substantially impaired." This reason for downward departure applies in this case because, by the process of elimination, there is no other explanation for the defendant's conduct.

The most important question that has remained unanswered since the trial of this case is, what caused Mary Hill to do what she did that resulted in the deaths and injuries to these children?

No one, not the State Attorney, nor anyone else who has knowledge of the facts and circumstances surrounding this case and the law that must be applied, has accused Mary Hill of murder. Indeed, the facts establish an absence of the intent necessary to sustain such a verdict. There is no evidence that Mary Hill awoke on August 2000, and sometime during that day decided to wreck her automobile with the children in it. And the jury rejected the possibility of mechanical failure. The only explanation left that has any basis in the record is the fact that she suffers from the various psychiatric and physical disorders described by the expert witnesses and these problems, while not excusing her reckless conduct, explain it.

If any of the two justifications for downward departure discussed above are found to be insufficient in themselves, they are sufficient when considered in combination and with the totality of the other circumstances in this case:

The legislature did not restrict the reasons for departure from the presumptive sentence to the reasons listed in the statute. The legislature recognized that the courts required the flexibility to use their discretion in unusual cases. This is one of those cases. The court finds that if any of the two justifications for downward departure discussed above are found to be insufficient in themselves, they are sufficient when considered in combination and with the totality of the other circumstances in this case.

There is no easy answer to the question of how to sentence the defendant for the crimes for which she has been convicted. No sentence will undo the harm done nor will it bring back the children that were so tragically lost on Markham Woods Road that day. No sentence imposed will heal the injuries the surviving child received. No sentence imposed will satisfy a basic sense of justice whether it be for the victims, their families, or the defendant.

This case has been the most publicized criminal case in Seminole County in recent years. It has been the subject of much discussion in the media and elsewhere. The tragic circumstances even drew the attention of national television. The court is aware of the desire for vengeance in this case on the part of some people and the desire for mercy on the part of others.

It is the duty of the courts to decide cases impartially and without the emotions that tragic circumstances arouse. And while courts seek to do justice, sometimes justice simply cannot be done. Certainly, in cases such as this one, it is better to fashion a sentence that will take into consideration the need for punishment of the defendant while taking into consideration all of the facts and circumstances in this case.

IT IS ADJUDGED:

The court will depart from the presumptive sentence in this case for the following reasons:

1. The offense was committed in an unsophisticated manner and was an isolated incident for which the defendant has shown remorse.

2. The capacity of the defendant to appreciate the criminal nature of the conduct or to conform that conduct to the requirements of law was substantially impaired.

3. If any of the justifications for downward departure listed above are found to be insufficient in themselves, they are sufficient when considered in combination and with the totality of the other circumstances in this case.

4. The extent of departure is not subject to appellate.

—O. H. Eaton Jr., Circuit Judge

CHAPTER 20

Where there is mystery, it is generally
suspected there must also be evil.
                              —Lord Byron

Just as it seemed the victims' families would be
able to try to move on with their lives, and try to make
peace with the tragedy as best they could, an appeal
for a new trial was filed. The mystery witness Darlene,
who had called Tim Berry's office before the sentencing, had finally made herself known.

The defense was granted a hearing to be held before
Judge Eaton on Friday, October 24, 2004. Berry was certain that the new witnesses—the mysterious, previously anonymous woman and her husband—would
have changed the outcome of the original trial if they
had testified. If the judge found in their favor, the
whole process would begin anew. . . . Mary Hill would
be tried again.

Although the new Seminole County Courthouse
was nearing completion, with some divisions already
moving in, the hearing was held at the previous site,
Judge Eaton's Courtroom B. If you have ever heard

the expression "The air was tingling with something," it was this day. It was tingling with frustration, jangled nerves *and* anticipation as everyone waited for the mystery woman to be called to testify.

Speculation was rampant. What could be the purpose of witnesses coming forward so long after the crash and the trial? Why had they not come forward earlier? Were they paid to appear? Did they have some agenda of their own? The defense would focus on what she, her husband and one son would testify that they saw on August 7, 2000. Prosecutor Pat Whitaker had finally taken time off to have back surgery. The prosecution, headed this time out by ASA Bart Schneider, would focus on discrepancies it found in the timeline and their testimony compared to the testimony of previous witnesses.

The first witness called was not Darline Chatman, the defense's mystery caller. The first witness called was her husband, Sheldry Chatman, whose nickname is Peewee. His style was definitely *Miami Vice*, wearing a black suit with an aqua T-shirt. Although average height, the African American man was powerfully built, giving the appearance of a weight lifter or perhaps a construction worker. He told Berry that he, accompanied by his wife, had picked up their two sons from the first day of school at Lake Mary High School. He said he saw the black BMW on Lake Mary Boulevard, as well as the white van. Directly contradicting Jimmy Arthur and Stan Philpot, Chatman said that while driving his family along Lake Mary Boulevard in his Chevy Silverado, he "picked up" the BMW somewhere near I-4, but he didn't know the time, as he seldom wore a watch. He said Hill was not driving recklessly or speeding. By the time the crash occurred, he said, he was directly behind Arthur's van, although he didn't know it was Arthur's van, on Markham Woods Road. He stopped only at his wife's insistence. He said he didn't want to get involved because of a bad accident he was in at the age of ten.

Chatman said that his wife said, "Stop. Stop." He pulled over and saw a man he knew, Stan Philpot, and went over and talked to him for a while. He said he talked to him the whole time they were there, leaving just before the law arrived.

He would say that he didn't come forward because of the media attention the case was attracting and he had not paid attention to the case, because he didn't read newspapers or watch television news—although walking by the TV, he would occasionally catch a "flash" of information about it.

When Bart Schneider cross-examined Chatman, he pointed out he had taken a deposition from him the previous day, where Chatman refused to answer some questions, including providing his home address. (In fact, when the state attorney's office had to later contact Chatman, its only resource was to contact Stan Philpot, after it was discovered he was related to Chatman by marriage. Philpot didn't have direct contact with Chatman, but let the message be known among family members.)

Schneider showed Chatman some documents, which became Exhibits E and F, with Chatman's name on them, revealing felony convictions. Chatman said they were his deceased brother's crime record, and that his brother had used his name instead of his own. "That one's not me," he said about one of the documents.

Schneider closely questioned him about the timing

of his arrival at the accident, which happened at 4:15 P.M., according to Jimmy Arthur's watch. Lake Mary High School let out at 2:00 P.M. Did he go anywhere else after picking up his sons? Why did it take him two hours to drive to the fatal crash on Markham Woods Road? It only took the Hills a much shorter time— from Greenwood Lakes Middle School, only a short distance from Lake Mary High, to travel nearly the same distance from a school releasing students at 3:50 P.M., and they had admittedly made a stop in between. Chatman couldn't account for the time difference, saying he made no stops.

Chatman did tell him that his mind was in a daze at the intersection, that he had a lot on his mind and didn't remember what happened on Markham Woods Road. He said he didn't see the crash.

Chatman told Schneider that now, for the first time in fifty years, he was in fear for his life and his family's safety. He and his family felt they were being targeted by SCSO. Schneider countered with demanding he be fingerprinted. He wanted to know if the felony convictions were actually his or his brother's. Tim Berry interceded, pointing out that Sheldry Chatman's fingerprints could be obtained for comparison with the felony-conviction records, to determine who was who.

When Darline Chatman (she spells it with an *i* instead of an *e*) was called to the stand, a conservatively dressed, attractive black woman walked purposefully to the front of the courtroom. She was sworn in and what would become a tension-bound first of three hearings— brought about because of her months-ago anonymous call—continued with her sworn testimony.

When Darline Chatman began her testimony, she told Berry and the court that her family had not wanted to get involved, and had left the scene of the crash before the arrival of law enforcement officers. When asked why they didn't come forward when it was apparent that Mary Hill was charged and brought to trial, her answer was that they didn't read newspapers or watch television newscasts, although they thought they heard something about the case at times.

She maintained they had been on Lake Mary Boulevard at the same time as Mary Hill, and had observed her and saw the car crash occur. The Chatmans' testimonies disputed the testimony of Jimmy Arthur, Stan Philpot and Earl Hodil, and Mary Hill herself, who admitted the car was speeding, only she said she wasn't causing it to speed.

The couple, Darline and Sheldry Chatman, and one of their two sons said Mary Hill was driving a normal speed the whole time, even though Mary herself said the car was speeding out of control on Markham Woods Road.

Darline Chatman didn't remember what time school was out at Lake Mary High, her sons had just started there and it was their first day. Later, they would say they were detained for a while by a meeting at the school. Residents of Apopka, the boys had previously been students at Lake Brantley High School. She said she transferred them to Lake Mary to get a better education for them.

Darline Chatman said Mary Hill was driving normally along Lake Mary Boulevard, passing their vehicle and pulling in front of a white van ahead of them. She said the light was red at the intersection, and she didn't notice anything unusual happening there. When they came upon the crash scene, she wanted her

husband to stop, but he didn't want to. She said her
sons were of driving age, and she wanted them to see
the accident. She saw Mary Hill on the ground, where
she had been ejected from the car, and saw the three
children in the backseat of the wrecked car. She
looked at them, then went back to Mary Hill, and said,
"God bless your family." At this time, she said Dennis
Hill came up and approached Mary, berating her,
though her recollection had none of the strong language that Arthur, Philpot and Mary Hill remembered him using. She said he said, "What have you
done now? What have you done now?"

She said she didn't come forward because she
didn't want the media "in her face, talking about her,
like Mary Hill" and looking into her background.
(She had a felony conviction for cocaine delivery
after a 1989 arrest.) Mary Hill's conviction was "just
on my mind," she said after admitting she was Tim
Berry's anonymous caller . . . She also answered why
there was no reply to his newspaper ad. By their own
admission, the Chatmans don't read newspapers. She
said, "I was afraid at first." She admitted she had been
convicted of a felony and she didn't want her children
questioned, because they were learning disabled.

She (and her husband) said they feared the sheriff's office because of problems they had with them.
Their boys were maced and hit with a blackjack, she
said, when she called them to help with her sons.

The sheriff's arrest report obtained through a search
of public records revealed a little more to the story. Darline Chatman called 911 on April 22, 2002, in a domestic dispute with one of her sons. While deputies
were en route to their Apopka apartment, the dispatcher reported hearing someone throwing things
inside the apartment and that a verbal disturbance

could be heard in the background. Darline Chatman told the dispatcher that she was stepping outside to get away from her son.

When SCSO deputy Theresa Brodersen arrived, she met with Darline Chatman, who was accompanied by husband Sheldry Chatman. Darline told her she was having a problem with two of her three sons. She told Deputy Brodersen that she couldn't handle them anymore and wanted them removed from her residence. When the deputy entered the apartment, she found three boys in the living room, all of whom Darline Chatman said were her sons. She pointed out the two she wanted removed from the home. When one of the sons refused to obey the deputy's requests, then actively resisted her, Brodersen administered a burst of O.C. spray, Oleoresin capsicum, commonly known as pepper spray. As he continued to resist while she attempted to handcuff him, she administered another burst of O.C. spray. Sheldry Chatman actively assisted the deputy in attempting to subdue the young man and tried to calm him, to no avail. It was only after the arrival of SCSO deputy Barry Brady that the youth, who was six feet tall and weighed 165 pounds, was finally restrained. He was taken to the Juvenile Assessment Center (JAC); thereafter, he was medically cleared of the O.C. exposure by the duty nurse at John E. Polk Correctional Facility, then was transported back to JAC.

Other SCSO reports, obtained through a search of public records, revealed further problems with some of her children. Because the documents had been redacted (the names marked out) of the juveniles involved, it was impossible to determine which sons were involved in each incident, but the reports support

Peewee Chatman's worries about his family having a
history with SCSO.

Bart Schneider asked Darline Chatman why had she
let Mary Hill sit in jail and prison for months, if she
knew she wasn't guilty. Her reply was "I didn't. They
are the ones who put her in jail." She didn't elaborate
on who "they" were.

In the meantime, Schneider had arranged for Lake
Mary High School principal Boyd Kearns to come to
court to confirm local dismissal times, since the Chatmans were sketchy about a timeline of when events
occurred. He confirmed that dismissal time for Lake
Mary High School on August 7, 2000, was 2:20 P.M. and
that he could drive the distance between Lake Mary
High and Greenwood Lakes Middle in fifteen minutes. Principal Kearn said that the dismissal time
that day at Greenwood Lakes was 3:50 P.M.

The defense called on Mary Hill, who had been
brought up from Homestead Correctional Institution,
in Homestead, to Sanford, to testify. In a tearful, low
voice, she told the court that when her husband,
Dennis, had arrived on the scene that day, he had
yelled at her and asked, "What the fuck have you
done now?" Amazingly, the main thing she remembered after more than four years was his abrasive behavior toward her. That was etched into her memory.

Judge Eaton continued the hearing to Monday,
November 1, 2004, as the defense had another witness
it wanted to call, and the prosecution wanted to
check out the Chatmans' background.

The November 1 hearing took place at the new
Seminole County Justice Center on Bush Boulevard.
It is a truly imposing building on US 17-92, across

from Flea World. The tall, classic, vaguely "Gothic-looking" (probably neoclassical) building peers down on the colorful buildings of the flea market across the street. People at the flea market are looking for fun; while those across the street look for justice.

Judge Eaton's new courtroom is Courtroom 5D. The waiting area outside the courtroom provides a splendid bird's eye view of the parking lot below and the sheriff's office to the left—the view is loftier than the one at the old courthouse, but not nearly as lovely.

The new courtroom is austere with upright specta-tor benches that look like church pews. They are not nearly as comfortable as the theater-style seating in the old courtroom. It is apparent there are people pres-ent for other hearings, other than the continuance of the Mary Hill appeal.

In short order, Judge Eaton announced the Mary Hill hearing will not be concluded today, because a state's witness had not yet appeared and would have to be subpoenaed, although some testimony would take place.

Rita Brown's parents, who were traveling in Florida, were present at the hearing, giving their daughter moral support.

The testimony heard that day was from Darline Chatman's son Henry Garden. A tall young man—in untied boots, blue jeans and an untucked blue shirt—he was very casually dressed for the occasion. He told the court that he saw Dennis Hill, at the crash scene, "run, slip and lost his balance, then regained it." He didn't remember exactly what Hill said, but it was something like "What the hell?" He had been sit-ting behind his mother in their truck and had watched Dennis Hill as he came up to the scene, screaming.

He was very hazy on a lot of other things that happened on that August 2000 day, but he clearly remembered a woman standing by a white fence and his mother making him go look at the children in the backseat of the car. He said his parents told him, "This is what happens when you don't wear seat belts." A strange comment, when one of the only two survivors wasn't wearing a seat belt and likely would have been killed if she had. All three children he was forced to view were wearing seat belts.

He told Schneider that in the four years that had passed, he had not talked to one person about the crash, until now. He was fourteen years old when the crash occurred.

The appeal brought everyone back into court for a final hearing on Tuesday, November 30, 2004. Mary Hill was present again, sitting in the otherwise vacant jury box. From her profile, she looked very much like the late serial killer Aileen Wuornos. It was probably the lack of makeup with her pale complexion, brown hair now growing out from the blond and pulled into a plain ponytail. Her prison jumper, worn over a long-sleeved white T-shirt or sweatshirt, completed the transformation. She looked tired and disinterested in the whole proceeding. She had the air of a woman who had given up. The whole atmosphere seemed different from previous hearings, almost a sense of boredom. A woman sitting on one of the "pews" was signing Christmas cards and addressing envelopes for them. Most of the people in the courtroom were either courtroom personnel or the media. A well-known investigative television reporter commented to a man from the sheriff's office, "All anyone needs is something else to happen in this case." Something else happening wouldn't be that day.

The missing state's witness from the last hearing for the appeal for a new trial, Stan Philpot, appeared. Prosecutor Bart Schneider shouldered the blame for the confusion of where he was supposed to be, and on what day, from the previous hearing. Philpot did not recall seeing the Chatmans at the crash scene, nor did he recall speaking to Peewee Chatman—something he likely would remember, as he is related to him in a fashion, through marriage. But before Philpot would take the stand, both FHP corporals Smith and Wright were called to testify. They stood by their previous testimony and crash report findings.

Tim Berry tried to discredit Jimmy Arthur's testimony (he was not present, as he moved to Auburn, California) when cross-examining Corporal Wright. Berry tried to get Wright to say there were inconsistencies in the interviews with Arthur. Wright replied that, overall, inconsistencies with a lay person often come up on what they did or what happened. "Your brain is going one hundred miles per hour," he said. It was not unusual in his experience, for people not to relate everything, every time interviewed, he assured Berry.

When Berry tried to get him to say it was a gross inconsistency, and pointed out that he had already challenged Wright's work on the case in court, Wright told him, "I let my record through thirty-three years stand for itself."

When Stan Philpot was asked to testify, Judge Eaton asked him, "You actually saw the crash occur?"

"Yes, sir" was his prompt reply. "I was there from the beginning to the end." He seemed very certain they weren't there or, at the very least, he didn't see them.

The defense called Christy Johnson, a woman who

was a neighbor of Debra Bejerkestrand's. She recalled hearing the sound of an accelerating engine, winding up and not backing off. Then she heard the impact. She looked out a window and saw a white van pulling off the road. She walked down to the south end of her property and saw the crashed BMW, the van and some people standing in a nearby backyard—at least two or three African Americans were standing there, walking around. She didn't remember them being on the same side of the road as the crash site.

Her neighbor Debra Bejerkestrand came over and the two went closer down to the road, about fifteen minutes after the crash happened. About the black people she remembered, she said, "In my mind, I see them on the Rays' side." (These were neighbor's living on the road across from the side where the crash occurred.)

Bejerkestrand was called to testify, but could relate nothing new, except that at the time she had a white fence and gate! She thought she remembered seeing a light-colored pickup truck, but she said, "The police were not there when I first arrived. A lot of people were there and vehicles on both sides [of the road]. I only remember lots of people. I couldn't identify them."

Christy Johnson was recalled and Peewee Chatman was brought in, but she couldn't identify him as being present at the crash scene.

In possibly the most startling event of the hearing, Tim Berry was called upon to testify, questioned by his assistant, attorney Paula Coffman. Although petite, she relentlessly pressed her point. The purpose of the Berry testimony was to discredit Arthur's previous testimony, an action Bart Schneider strenuously objected to. Coffman pressed the team's point—that Arthur's testimony got better and better as time went on.

In the end, Judge Eaton declared the purpose of the hearing was to relate newly discovered evidence, not to go over what had been presented in the past.

Judge Eaton ruled the testimony of the new witnesses, the Chatmans, would not have changed the outcome of the trial. He felt they were actually there, from the many details they knew and were able to relate, but what they said wouldn't have made any difference in the outcome of the trial. The motion for a new trial was denied.

Rita Brown and both the Rockwells could only express a feeling of relief that they would not have to go through a new trial and could possibly get on with their lives. But there was still an appeal to be heard by the Fifth District Court of Appeal in Daytona, possibly sometime in spring 2005. A Notice of Appeal was filed on January 7, 2005, and the appellee (Mary Hill) was ordered to pay a $300 filing fee, which was waived in mid-February when she was declared insolvent. Defense team attorney Paula Coffman, whose forte is appeals, will represent Mary Hill, and the Attorney General's Office of the State of Florida will represent the state. Each side will be allowed fifteen minutes to speak. Then it will be over, or start again.

Defense attorney Tim Berry said he was still convinced of Mary Hill's innocence. He said he continued the pursuit of the out-of-control cruise control defense, because as a former BMW owner, a similar thing happened to him with his cruise control. "I have sat with her while she has wept over the death of those two children. I don't believe for a moment she did it intentionally," he said. Berry said there is a third possibility of what happened, speculating, "She simply had her foot on the accelerator and not on the brake, and fully believed she was braking when she was accelerating." Driver error. "But [that] is negated by the fact that the only truth James Arthur told, as far as I am concerned, is that he saw the brake lights come on. That is backed up by the witnesses that came forward later and by the passenger in the van, Stanford Philpot." Berry absolutely believed the crash was just a tragic accident.

Berry talked a little about Mary Hill's previous representation before he took over the case. "Her first attorney was Jim Russ, who is probably one of the most incredible lawyers in the state, and in this country," said Berry. "For some reason, that I can only speculate about, her counsel was changed to Mr. Boyle (Gerald) by Mr. Hill. Mr. Boyle, who is not licensed to practice law in Florida, retained Mr. Culhane so he could practice (acting as an adviser), so they were in the case for a while. Mr. Culhane then decided to go back and be a prosecutor again and then Mr. Boyle and I worked together briefly on the case, and Mrs. Hill determined she wanted to discharge Mr. Boyle, and here I am." Berry was the only attorney that Mary Hill hired, the other attorneys were hired by Dennis Hill.

It was Berry's understanding, as had been revealed by others close to the case, that Dennis Hill had been intent upon suing BMW. Berry said he was never involved in that, garnering a lot of hostility from Dennis Hill and Gerald Boyle when he got into the case, "but that died down."

Berry laughed at the thought that Dennis Hill was broke, as he was telling Kaitlynn and the Wilsons. What was known was that Mary Hill was destitute and could not even pay the court costs associated with the sentence. Judge Eaton ruled that she could pay the fine and court costs in fifty-four equal payments while on probation. (It was likely, although he did not say so, that Berry and his team have been representing Mary Hill gratis through the last hearings.) "I am just amazed that the court has allowed him to drag this out for as long as he has," he said about the situation with Kaitlynn and the Wilsons.

"Mrs. Hill has had a lot of terrible things happen to her in her life. She had these mental-health issues, and at some point she abused prescription drugs. But it's very clear to me that on this day, when this accident happened, she wasn't on drugs, she wasn't on alcohol, she had just seen a psychiatrist—I mean, it's the defense lawyer's dream. And yet . . . I am convinced if we had tried this case in Iowa, if we had tried this case in South Florida, she would have walked out of that courtroom a free person. I think that just four years of all this negative publicity permeated the jury," Berry said. "I am just devastated by the verdict.

"One good thing came out of the final hearing. Judge Eaton said he believed our witnesses. He found them to be credible and he believed that they were there. That is one judgment that the district court of appeals cannot make. They can't determine the credibility of witnesses they don't hear or see. Now they just have to decide if the judge was correct in his ruling. Hopefully, they will do the right thing. I think there was reasonable doubt."

CHAPTER 21

You don't develop courage by being happy in your
relationships every day. You develop it by surviving
difficult times and challenging adversity.

—Epicurus

On January 4, 2005, Washington Mutual, the mort-
gager on the Hills' fabulous mansion, sold the property on the courthouse steps in Sanford—the same
courthouse where Mary Hill's trial was held nearly a
year prior to the sale.

Today, Mary Hill is incarcerated at Homestead Correctional Institution in Homestead, Florida, a maxi-
mum-control women's prison, where she works as
dustman, cleaning up the dormitory where she resides.

Her daughter Kaitlynn Hill seems to be flourishing
under the care of her other daughter Jennifer and her
son-in-law Michael Wilson. The Wilsons continue to
struggle with Dennis Hill in family court.

"My mom is doing well," said Jennifer Wilson.
"When I visited her—it took me a while, I refused at
first. I couldn't write her a letter. I couldn't talk to her
on the phone. I just couldn't bear it. There's the

sadness, the embarrassment, I guess you would say. I know that sounds selfish, but she's my mom. She's not the stereotypical inmate you think of being in prison.

"I finally did get down there and I couldn't even make it in. Then I tried again, and got in and I left. Then I tried again and she couldn't be seen, then Kaitlynn and I just actually went just a few weeks ago, we went and saw her [between Thanksgiving and Christmas 2004] and that's the only time we've seen her since the sentencing. There was not a stitch of makeup on her and she was just in her prison clothes, and I don't remember my mom looking that good in a very long time.

"She said she felt better, she knew this was where she needed to be. She would have died if she wasn't there. If she would have been at home, she would be dead right now. And you know, of course, she feels fully responsible and she needs to pay for what she has done, which I don't agree. I know, I mean fifteen years? You can kill somebody out on the street and only get seven. If there is time to be spent, I agree, but don't think it needs to be fifteen years, absolutely not. The gentleman that said all that stuff about her driving erratically down the road, you know he was there that day and never gave any of those statements until two years later, those statements came out. To this day, nobody can find him. They have ordered him to court, and they have put out subpoenas for him and he won't show up in court anymore.

"She looks healthy now. I don't know if Kaitlynn remembers Mom like I do, the fun, giving person. She is about the most giving person you will ever meet. There was a lady she met at a horse show once, that was in terrible trouble, and she just gave her money to help her get out [of it]. She was just that kind of person. She would do anything for you and give anything.

"She got lost somehow. Not that her unhappiness was an excuse, but nobody would help her. When you reach that point, it should be your family structure that helps you. There should be somebody who loves you enough to bring you back. If attempts were made and they failed, then there would be a terrible tragedy there. But no attempts were made. No one came to her aid to help her. She was just left to deteriorate. You know what? Deterioration was easier to deal with—because the fight was hard, and she was out of the way of other things that were going on. The healthy Mary would get pissed off that life was not the way it should be, whereas the drug-induced Mary was too drugged to care and became materialistic, because that's what happens to addicts, because they start thinking about things to help maintain [the addiction].

"She couldn't bear what happened, the loss of her child. She tried to drink it away after the accident. And she just wanted to die, and I can't really blame her for that. I was still very active, trying to get somebody to help. I couldn't be there. I tried to call who I could. I tried to Baker Act my mom [to have her involuntarily committed to a hospital for mental evaluation]. I tried to get her some help. Nobody would help me."

Nearing Christmas, 2004, Keith and Zak Rockwell walked up to Rita Brown's home with their dogs, Lucky, a golden retriever, and Brittany, an old English sheepdog. The two dogs pressed their noses up against the front door as they watched Astro running around inside the house. He was visiting with Mel Stevens, with whom he now lives. Jennifer Brown was visiting from California for the holidays. The five friends sat down together around Rita Brown's dining-room table, drawn together as only people who have endured tragedy together can be.

Zak Rockwell was "getting on" with his life. He refurbished a 1968 Cadillac Coupe de Ville, then sold it, buying himself a 2002 Chevrolet Avalanche, which he had customized with a new sound system and twenty-two-inch wheels. He has been pursuing his athletic interests in motocross, dirt biking and surfing, and acoustic guitar as well. He enjoys jamming with popular acoustic songs. An honor roll student, he is currently trying to decide upon universities to attend. He thinks he would like to pursue a business degree; although at present, he isn't quite sure what he will do with that knowledge.

Keith Rockwell, as his name implies, has stood behind his son, giving him the "rock" he has needed, to get to the point of independence he has now reached. Zak and his mother, Mary, who moved to California from her New Smyrna Beach home, talk on the phone every day.

Although Rita Brown and Mel Stevens have seemingly ended their personal relationship, they have remained friends and business associates. Rita was still very aware of fun-loving Carrie's presence. "Whenever I pass the oak tree where the crash occurred, if I am talking on my cell phone, the phone goes dead. Every time." Occasionally she or Jennifer will feel the familiar tug at her elbow. They both know it's Carrie making her presence known. Everyone, including Mary Hill, would like to believe Carrie is holding Amy's hand, giving her the same love and support she always did when they were here.

Oddly enough, probably the only two people who are at peace are Carrie and Amy, the two victims of a "speed demon."

ACKNOWLEDGMENTS

It is impossible to thank everyone who has given so freely of time and knowledge while I was researching *Speed Demon*. The support offered by many people involved in all aspects of this case was overwhelming.

Notable were the contributions from victims' families, the Browns and Rockwells. It took much courage to relive situations they had hoped to place behind them. I am grateful they were willing, one more time, to relive a tumultuous four years. Not only did they share information—they were generous with photographs as well.

I would be remiss if I did not thank Jennifer Wilson, Mary Hill's oldest daughter. To me, she proved herself to be a sensitive, courageous woman. When looking for a role model, her younger sister could do no better than Jennifer. I wish both of them well. My personal opinion is, the two surviving children of Mary Hill may well be the two people who will be her saving grace.

I owe appreciation to Gary Roen, who introduced me to the folks at Kensington Publishing Corp., and gratitude to them for accepting me despite my eccentricities.

Thanks must also be given to Dr. Leon James, aka

Dr. Driving, nationally recognized expert in the field of road rage and aggressive driving, who kindly allowed me use of some of his research in this book. His Web site (www.drdriving.org) offers valuable insight into this growing national problem. He has published extensively on the subject and has testified before Congress, recognized as *the* expert on the subject. Take a test on his Web site and find out what type of driver you are.

Shug Norgren, my critique partner, who is such a great "sounding board," deserves more than thanks for holding my hand and giving me great advice, even when we were both in panic mode, trying to survive the three successive hurricanes that hit both our homes this season.

Thank you to my family, especially Jim, for always believing in me and encouraging me to follow my heart, even when it meant spending hours researching and writing, instead of spending time with them. Lastly, thanks to Himself and Fu—who for a Milk-Bone each—will agree anything I write is golden.

AUTHOR'S NOTE

Crime seems to change character when
it crosses a bridge or tunnel . . .
                            —Barbara Ehrenreich

Ehrenreich, a social critic and essayist, proposes that crime in the city (over a bridge or through a tunnel) is seen more as a product of "class and race" but it is perceived differently when it takes place in the suburbs. She describes it as a "mystery of the individual soul" that changes, escaping causation, generalizations of just class or just race. She says crime in the suburbs becomes intimate; it becomes psychological.

Speed Demon uses no "fictionalization" to tell its story. It is told through research of hundreds of pages of sworn depositions, trial testimonies, many hours of author interviews with key participants, and perusing an incredible amount of court and law enforcement records.

The names of some individuals in this account have been changed to help protect their privacy and/or careers. All except one are employees or former employees of the Hills' research empire. With those named, it was necessary to change the names of a few people not interviewed, to protect the identities of all. The interviewees fear reprisal within the national marketing research community if their true identities are revealed. Interviewed individually, they each confirmed details related by the others.

Some comments of Mary Hill and Dennis Hill were taken from sworn depositions and their trial testimony. Dennis Hill has refused numerous offers to be interviewed.

People told me the same, or very similar, stories. Some of them may have had some details "a little off," or not in the appropriate time frame, but so many people were giving the same basic information about many different things that had happened within the Hill family that it was not to be ignored.

An offer was also made to Mary Hill through her attorney to be interviewed. The only person to "speak" for the Hill family is Mary Hill's oldest daughter, Jennifer Wilson. She is a forthright young woman who has managed to cope and triumph despite the misfortune life seems to have dealt her. The state of Florida has given custody of Kaitlynn, her younger half sister, the surviving daughter of Dennis and Mary Hill, to her and her husband, Michael Wilson.

Although the victims in this book are children, their names have become public through extensive media coverage and trial testimony. Other children have also become known through court documents and/or media reports. There is no intent on the part of the author to cause them any embarrassment, or to exploit them in any manner, by the use of their names. In view of past publicity naming them, it would be senseless to attempt to preserve their anonymity here. The names of some people and businesses have become known through information publicly available through law enforcement files, sworn depositions, testimony and other material available under freedom of information laws. Others have become known through media attention. Their names have been used as critical to advancing the story, although some individuals or entities either elected not to be interviewed by the author.

Reports, psychological evaluations entered as evidence and summaries used in *Speed Demon* were readily available in court files for anyone making a public-record request.

This story has not ended. On many levels, it is only beginning. I can only hope and pray that everyone involved comes out of it a survivor as the remainder of the story plays to a conclusion.

I truly believe that the portion of the story I have revealed is only the climax—the compound tragedy of the deaths of Carrie Brown and Amy Hill, the injury of Zak, the disintegration of at least three families and the subsequent conviction and imprisonment of Mary Hill. The end is yet to be played out.

I would be remiss if I did not advise readers, if you know of any people caught up in an addiction of any kind, or who have become victim to domestic violence, persist in getting them help. They and their loved ones—enablers or abusers—may be in absolute denial of their situation. They may refuse your help, but somewhere, at some point, someone will listen. There are many local community agencies that will supply information about obtaining help. If you are at a loss as to where to begin looking for help, most phone directories list community help agencies in specially coded pages. If your phone directory doesn't list that information, call your local health department, a help line, or even the sheriff's office, they should be able to give you some guidance. Your help may not be welcomed—addicts and victims often do not recognize that they need help. If they are aware of their problems, they often don't realize help is available to them. Addicts, however, may not want help, and victims of abuse often think they are the ones at fault. Your concern may avert tragedy and, at least, you will know you did all you could do.

If you are addicted, depressed or abused yourself, please seek help. You may not think, or may have been told, you are not worth saving. Perhaps you have been told you are at fault for your troubles, often people will try to make you feel guilty for seeking help. You are worth saving. Save yourself—you can do it! Look in the telephone directory or call information, ask for a mental-health hot line. There are people who will help you. Don't give up.

EPILOGUE

In a case that has experienced more bends and twists than the nearby St. Johns River, Mary Hill walked out of prison ten and a half months after being incarcerated—not completely a free woman, but close to it for the present.

Paula Coffman, the attorney who is handling her appeal before the district appeals court, presented a motion to Judge O. H. Eaton asking to grant a Supersedeas Bond/Stay of Sentence pending the outcome of the appeal.

In his order granting the bond, Judge Eaton wrote that at first he was inclined to deny the bond, but after some research, he changed his mind.

In the State of Florida, granting of such a bond pending appeal is based on both "statute and by court decision." Mary Hill's convictions are not on "the list" of convictions that would prohibit the court granting such a bond. She had no previous felony convictions before the conviction on appeal and no other felony charges pending, so Coffman's request was seriously considered. In a five-page order, Eaton weighed the pros and cons, elaborating on how he arrived at his decision.

Coffman originally requested that Hill be released on $1,000 bond because the court had found her indigent in regards to the expenses of her appeal. Judge Eaton set the bond at $50,000. The State vehemently objected to the motion to release Hill. Late Friday afternoon, June 17, 2005, Coffman contacted her client at Homestead Correctional Institutution (HCI) in Homestead, Florida and told her she could get out of jail, but not for free.

In another one of the twists to the ongoing case, Mary Hill was rescued from prison by her estranged husband, Dennis Hill. While Mary Hill resided at HCI, her divorce attorney continued the fight to force Dennis Hill to reveal what assets he possessed and how others had been disposed of. Dennis's attorney wrote the court stating that her client had "suffered significant financial devastation and has lost his business," as Jennifer and Mike Wilson continued to battle Dennis for child support. She further informed the court that Dennis was "currently on unemplyment and is simply unable to pay the child support ordered."

The past animosity didn't stop Dennis from rescuing his wife. He secured the bail and brought Mary Hill home to his house in the exclusive, gated community of Heathrow Country Club, a short distance from their former residence.

Rita Brown, who still lives in Wingfield North, said she was "shocked, amazed and confused" at the turn of events. She and a companion turned away from the door of a favorite restaurant when she recognized Dennis Hill's car in the parking lot. She said if she encountered Mary Hill elsewhere in the community, she would just turn and walk alway.

"We opposed her release on bond pending the outcome of the appeal; however, that decision was within the judge's discretion. We are confident the guilty verdict and sentence will be upheld on appeal. All this means is that she will be older when she completes her sentence than she would have been if she had continued to serve her time. Our sincere hope is that no one else is hurt in the interim," said State Attorney Norm Wolfinger.

Meantime, Mary Hill waits to find out if the court will impose any more restrictions on her freedom. The judge's order instructed her to stay in the county that she chose to reside in, not to drive and to report to the sheriff's office once a week. In an upcoming scheduled hearing, the State is asking that much stricter guidelines be set.